A PARENT'S STRENGTH . . .

What I knew the night of Don's death was that the lives of these two children were all that was left of the man I loved. I was thankful that I had them because without them I would want to die, too, rather than face the future alone. Even with them the future looked bleak. We would not always remain calm in the days and weeks to come. Together we would grieve over our loss. My children had become mourning children.

LINDA ALDERMAN holds a B.A. in psychology from the University of Michigan, and an M.A. in child development and family relations from the University of Connecticut. She has formed and facilitated groups for widowed parents in New Jersey and Michigan, lectured to parents and children on coping with death in the family, and appeared on television and radio programs. Formerly a teacher of psychology at Trenton State College in New Jersey, she now lives in Michigan.

"Tender, compassionate, insightful . . . *Why Did Daddy Die?* is an indispensable book for parents, teachers, and all professionals. I cried. I learned from its pages."
—RABBI EARL A. GROLLMAN, D.D.,
author of *Talking About Death:
A Dialogue Between Parent and Child*

"Linda Alderman tells a captivating story which is heroic and inspirational. . . . Her message is powerful."
—SANDRA L. GRAVES, Ph.D., ATR.
Director, American Grief Academy
of ACCORD, Inc.

WHY DID DADDY DIE?

Helping Children Cope with the Loss of a Parent

Linda Alderman

POCKET BOOKS

New York   London   Toronto   Sydney   Tokyo   Singapore

Another *Original* publication of POCKET BOOKS

POCKET BOOKS, a division of Simon & Schuster
1230 Avenue of the Americas, New York, NY 10020

ISBN: 0-671-74670-7

First Pocket Books trade paperback printing October 1989

10 9 8 7 6 5 4 3 2

POCKET and colophon are trademarks
of Simon & Schuster

Printed in the U.S.A.

*This book is dedicated to
the mourning child.*

ACKNOWLEDGMENTS

A simple thank you to . . .

Family members: Keith and Louise Baughman; Fred and Selma Alderman; Barbara, Mel, Andy, and Tammy Kahn; Ron Kramer; Steffa Harrison.

Those who helped support us in our grief: Dr. Franco Muggia; Dr. Nicholas Cifelli; Danny, Melissa, Jason, and Megan Kaden; Ken, Sharon, Paul, and Julie Skowronek; Gordon and Benita Hale; Susan Randolph Dean; Les Pittle; Karen and Emily Dunn; Sam and Ellen Offen; Penny, Chad, and Grant Riley; B. J. Rohrbacher; Wendy Freed.

Those who helped as we built a new life, either with support and companionship or in the preparation of this book: Elaine Pfefferblit; Natalie Chapman ("Natalie would like that!"); Carol Mann; Joe Healy; THEOS; Earl Grollman; Dan Jonkoff; Mary Knight; Lija Ditmar; Barbara McIntyre; Mary Raymer; Nancy Boynton Fisher; Richard and Carol Anderson; Dave, Lynn, Michael, and Benjamin Troutman; Erik, Ben, and Joe Shipman; all of my children's teachers; Dick and Liz Pomeroy; Millie and Mike Pyle; Donna Pollock; and especially the members of the widowed parents and art therapy support groups and my church.

Marc and Lara Alderman, the true authors of this book.

My husband, Dan, and children, Shan, Maya, and Chay. Even though you did not all appear in this book, I am forever grateful to God that you appeared in my life.

CONTENTS

INTRODUCTION

This book takes only a few hours to read, but the grieving process chronicled herein filled months and even years. It was necessary to compress events to clarify the three main threads of this book: first, my personal story, second, advice, and third, the theories of children's concepts of death and the phases of grief.

I have attempted for the ease and interest of the reader to keep this book in the order in which events actually occurred, but there were times, in discussing the theories, when examples had to be plucked from the past or future. The theory of children's concepts of death is presented early in the book to aid the reader's understanding of the mourning process for children, even though much of my knowledge was gained from the perspective of hindsight after listening to my children for over two years. My insight into children's experience with death and grief continues to expand to this day and beyond!

When the book's narrative continues, after illustrative time warps and theoretical digressions, the reader is then placed back into the chronological order of events. This approach seemed to make the book most readable, but I want to caution the reader that in grief, things do not happen in an orderly, chronological fashion. Grief unfolds very slowly for both children and adults. The journey is long. Be patient. Listen. Cry. Embrace. Heal. And grow.

EXCERPTS FROM A
Father's Journal

To my children:

Today was not an exceptional day except that I began a diary for you. Your mother started writing to you even before you were born, writing about our dreams and hopes and disappointments. Now I'm moved to write to you, too, because I don't want to wait until you are old enough to understand my thoughts. Although I'll be here to talk to you tomorrow and the next day and the day after, there won't be enough days for me to share myself with you. Some days I'll probably just let pass and others I'll not see. I've no idea when you might read this—how old either of you will be and why you will read it. But this will be my way of holding some letters for you.

I am sitting downstairs in our study. Your hamster, Scotchie, is rustling around in his cage, keeping me company as I write. The fruit trees around our home are in blossom in pink, white, and red, and I know their colors better than their expected fruits. I have been more prone to sit and read or write than to cultivate a garden or weed a lawn. Your dad does more with his head than with his arms or body.

Today was also the last day of my first cycle of chemotherapy treatments for cancer. I'm still not very good at handling this trauma—my hand is shaking as I put it into words. But I discovered that these treatments will affect me very much—not so much physically in terms of pain or illness, but emotionally. One of the drugs, prednisone, is a steroid that leads to hyperactivity. I was awake most of last night, and when you, Marc, came in to me for a hug, a morning welcome, I chased you away because I was too tired. Your mother assured me a few days won't undo our years of love, but I am saddened and hurt. I could tolerate the chemotherapy stealing a little from my work, my days, my health, and maybe even from the marriage that has made me grow and given my life real warmth and direction. But I can't let it change my relationship with my children. I am your father and you are my children. It is not a bond of power or ownership. It is a most special bond of love.

===== MAY 1980 =====

Yesterday I returned home from a business trip to New Orleans. I was touched when, after excitedly showing me a new toy, Marc said simply, "I missed you, Daddy." I missed you, too, Marc, but I also take you and Lara wherever I go.

===== MAY 1980 =====

It was a good weekend. This morning as I was replacing the bathroom light fixture, Marc asked me if I was glad that I had a son. I said yes and he explained that he was very glad to have a father. I hope reading this, when he is older, gives him a glimpse of how much our relationship means to me.

As I was mowing the lawn on our riding tractor this evening, Linda came out to tell Marc it was time to get ready for bed. He began to cry and said he wanted to ride with me on the tractor and have me push him on the swing. It was more than just postponing bed; he wanted us to spend a little time together at the end of the day. So he climbed into my lap and drove the tractor, as has become habit after each lawn mowing, and then I pushed him on the swing. I wonder who enjoys our time together more. No matter, it's precious to both of us.

Friday I start my second cycle of chemotherapy, so I can't expect much next weekend. But I have four full days before Friday. It's a lot easier to be optimistic and enjoy each day while off the drugs and free from their side effects. And you know, I haven't had a nightmare in a few nights. I had awakened from dreams about losing my hair, about hemorrhaging in my left arm, about the foundations of the house becoming an emptiness of mud and dark space. That last one seemed a clear parallel to my fears of mortality and concern for Marc, Lara, and Linda. It really scared me. But I am free from the drugs and full of awareness of my family.

================ JUNE 1980 ================

It has been three weeks and a treatment cycle since I made an entry in this journal. I find it hard to write while on the chemotherapy, and the last cycle left me tired each night. I still notice or have become overly sensitive to effects that impinge upon us as a family. When Linda becomes impatient after a long day, I regret that I can't or haven't tried to lessen her burden. I wish the emotional strain were less.

================ JUNE 1980 ================

Today was Father's Day. After a day of celebration Linda took Marc upstairs to get ready for bed while Lara and I played in the family room. I amused her, and she had me laughing with her impish smiles and giggles. Marc came downstairs in his pajamas and joined us. He told Linda and me that he wanted Lara to grow up so she could become his best friend. It warmed us to hear him speak with love and kindness about La. For many children a sibling is too much competition. I think he understands that his baby sister does not represent competition for our affection—that our love for both children is constantly growing.

When I tucked him in, Marc asked me to read him one of his books, about a son and father going camping, Just Me and My Dad. After I had read it, he hugged me and told me that he loved me. It made my Father's Day. This summer we'll all go camping.

JUNE 1980

I called and arranged my next appointment for chemotherapy after avoiding the call for over a week. I am having serious difficulty tolerating the treatments psychologically. It takes unusual determination and resignation to surrender yourself to such strong toxic agents knowing their effects and knowing that otherwise you would feel well.

As I make progress relating my tales of woe, I think I'm also making progress in learning to cope a little better. I still think about my motivation for keeping this journal. Besides wanting to communicate my thoughts to you children, I'm also recording them for myself. I can be honest on these pages and make admissions I might otherwise not express. So the journal is therapy for me as I wrestle with chemotherapy, mortality, the relative values of family, health, work, responsibilities to others, the incredible human animal, and other mysteries and unsolvable dilemmas. But know that even in the midst of crisis, you children bring me joyous days.

I have a treatment coming on Linda's birthday. And on the weekend Star Wars II, the movie I'd looked forward to taking Marc to, is in town. Damn. Knowing that the effects spread throughout a family makes cancer treatments more difficult.

DECEMBER 1980

It's been over six months since I made an entry. We went camping for the first time last summer. We spent our vacations in Michigan and in California for your cousin Andy's Bar Mitzvah. We had both sets of grandparents and Aunt Steffa for Thanksgiving dinner. I had a transfusion and got hepatitis, and the chemotherapy has stopped. The chemotherapy has stopped. The chemotherapy has stopped! It seems hard to believe.

MAY 1981

Two days after my last entry I received a telephone call from the oncologist in New York. The tumor had grown since the cessation of chemotherapy. After trying other treatments, I began radiation therapy last week.

I know that I've got to take hold of each day—like riding on the lawn mower with both children again today or taking them to the swim club last weekend—but I can't seem to regain my determination.

I depend very much on Linda's support and optimism. She has been the emotional pillar for all of us. The worst part for me is the irrational feeling that if the therapy isn't successful, I won't be Marc's or Lara's father or Linda's husband any more. How I want to watch my children grow up and enjoy the years with Linda.

SEPTEMBER 1981

I'm overly sensitive and probably irrational sometimes in this fight. Maybe I need to regain more of my independence and own strength, and rely less on Linda. Sometimes it seems that Linda has begun to rely less on me in raising you children, which I fear is part necessity because of my illness.

But who can I turn to when the fight becomes so hard? Maybe my simple and complete love for Marc and Lara.

I don't harbor any occupational expectations for either of you. Above all else I want you to be happy and healthy adults. I suppose that it would disappoint me if you didn't use your talents and energies, and stretch toward some goal or dream. I hope someday to share my accomplishments with you and you'll know that I tried to make a contribution.

I wish it weren't true, but now I know that the past months have taken a toll on my relationships with those closest to me. The anxiety and absence have worked upon us. I hope there will be time for mending. I love you, Tiger. I love you, La.

SEPTEMBER 1981

This evening I was thinking about the day I returned from that business trip to New Orleans over a year ago. I'd missed Linda, especially when I found the "I love you" note she'd slipped into my luggage, and I'd missed you children. For some reason, all the little pleasures of that first day home are still vivid in my memory.

I'd brought Marc a T-shirt with "New Orleans" written

on it and colorful pictures of a steamboat, the Superdome, and other attractions. Marc was so pleased when I gave it to him before breakfast that he immediately took off his pajama top and wore the shirt to preschool. Needless to say, I took pleasure in his joy. That was also the morning he signed his own name on the Mother's Day cards for his grandmothers. Very carefully he printed each letter of his first name and the first letter of his last name. Watching him sit at the kitchen table and work on printing his name in crayon on his own cards for the first time made me very proud. He'd had quite a bit of trouble with letters earlier that year when he started preschool, but neither Linda nor I felt it appropriate to make any special efforts. We knew he would learn and master new activities, like signing greeting cards in crayon.

Linda had collected small, pretty flowers with you children in the yard and then pressed them in wax paper, so you had your own gifts to send with the cards to your grandmothers. Few parents would devote the time, energy or creativity to such projects. I thought at the time how your mother daily renews my confidence and reinforces my choice of a wife. The pressed flowers were very special presents because you made them.

Lara had impressed me that day, too. When I'd come home from work she had watched me kiss Marc, then toddled over and said, "Kiss."

Good night, Marc. Good night, Lara. I love you. Dream about little pressed flowers for grandmothers. Dream about new accomplishments as a child prints his name in crayon. Dream about the light in a daughter's eyes as she says "Kiss" and the smile on a son's lips as he puts on a colorful souvenir shirt. And I hope my nightmares yield to your dreams.

Why Did Daddy Die?

*L*IFE BEFORE DEATH

No one ever said to us, "There is nothing more that can be done for you. Prepare yourselves. Prepare your children. Don is going to die." Perhaps no one wanted to take away our hope. After my husband died, I told his oncologist what a shock Don's death was to the children and to me, even though his cancer had been progressing for two years. "Where there is life, there is hope," he answered.

There definitely was life for the four of us even in the midst of the debilitating treatment that Don endured in an attempt to preserve that life.

Our son, Marc, was only three months old when Don's Hodgkin's disease was discovered after a routine chest x-ray. Three months later, when Don was hospitalized for tests and exploratory surgery to determine whether his malignancy had metastasized, I began to get a glimpse of how his cancer treatment would become a thread so tightly woven into our family life that it seemed almost normal to us, at least to the children. Life had always included Daddy's cancer treatment. Yet we clung to the hope that someday the children would have a healthy father.

Don's family was the most important part of his life. His greatest joy was the birth of our children, and the happiness of fatherhood never wore off. Don's cancer was discovered only months after our first child was born. During the initial period of despair over the shocking blow he'd been dealt, Don clung to the belief that as long as he could be with his son, his life had a purpose. Marc's visits to Don's hospital room during that first period of treatment in 1976 made such a difference in Don's mood. Surely someone who was needed so much by his child would be allowed to be there for that child. Don expected only what was fair, what was his right as a father. Marc was a big part of Don's hope.

Marc's presence helped make Don's hospitalization more pleasant in another way, too—the nurses on that particular floor loved babies. Don got even more attention because he was Marc's father. They took Marc for short walks so that Don and I could be alone together for a few precious moments. Marc, never shy with strangers, enjoyed the attention. On his sixth-month birthday several of the nurses brought him an ice cream cup tied with a bright ribbon and sang "Happy Birthday" to our pleasantly surprised little family.

The staff's kindness resulted from the way Don treated them. Because he respected the nurses as individuals, they were inspired to give a little more. Don related to people based on their strength of character and goodness, not on what position they occupied in the hierarchy. That made it easier for him not to be so intimidated by the numerous doctors and technicians who passed judgment on his body. The staff also appreciated Don's sense of humor, which allowed Don to endure the posing, prodding, and prepping for procedures, and other indignities of medical care.

When Don's initial hospital treatment was over, we were able to put the pain and suffering behind us. The only physical side effect during Don's remission was a low sperm count, which restored itself to normal in about a year and a half. When I became pregnant for a second time, we were sure that our lives were back to normal.

Because of my pregnancy, I decided to take a leave of absence from my part-time job of teaching child psychology at a local college. Don had a promising position as a research psychologist for one of the major producers of educational tests in the country. When we took out the mortgage on our dream house in Lambertville, New Jersey, we signed a chunk of his paycheck away until 1999, but my salary was still only gravy. Compared to our lean graduate-student days, we felt as though we had everything we wanted—with riches to spare. In fact, after our daughter, Lara, was born a neighbor commented that now we had a "rich man's family." We had the typical, all-American family of four.

Lara was a perfectly healthy baby, but her birth unexpectedly acquainted me with a part of life that I usually avoided pondering—death. Minutes after Lara was born I hemorrhaged and went into shock. Holding our baby, Don looked on as the entire obstetrical staff worked to stop me from bleeding to death.

At first I felt chilled. A nurse covered my shivering body with blankets. My surroundings became foggy. I was conscious, but I was not afraid of what was happening to me. It almost seemed as if the body being massaged and injected was not mine. I felt no pain. Like an astronaut in a zero-gravity chamber, I felt suspended in time and space. The possibility of dying never entered my disoriented thoughts. I was, in fact, quite serene. Eventually I came out of the fog to tell everyone that I was all right, that I was back with them again.

Later the incident seemed both frightening and comforting to me. Any brush with death is frightening. But after my own experience, I was less scared by the actual process of dying. I had to believe that death might not be the same for the dying person as for those people watching a loved one die.

By the time Lara was a year old, however, my serenity was wiped out by the terror that ripped through me when Don came home one evening and told me his routine checkup had shown a recurrence of Hodgkin's disease. For several days I hid my fear for the benefit of my husband and my two young children. The full comprehension of what might be ahead for us finally sunk in on the day Don and I stood on a train platform in Newark, on our way home from the first of many consultations with specialists over the next two years.

After trudging up the steep stairs, Don and I stood on the empty platform waiting for our train. Across a chasm of tracks another platform filled with people. The *why* hit me again. Why did we have to be the ones to face this terrible burden? Where would I get the strength to get through this ordeal, let alone to give to Don and my children? Tears streaked my face as I watched those other commuters board their train. They were going home free while we were left waiting alone. Don looked at me, understanding completely what I was feeling. We had been married for about ten years. He put his arm around me and said what I had so often said to him, "Don't worry, Hon. Everything will be all right. We'll get through it together. I love you."

Because he believed it, so did I. Don had reminded me where my strength came from—from him and his love. For just a moment he could protect me with his encircling arm from the disappointment of life as later when that arm was too weak to raise, he would give me strength with a smile or a light touch. Thank you for being the strong one when I really needed you, Don.

That day at the train station wasn't the first or the last time I wondered at the almost mystical way we were able to balance each other's need for support. Our technique of pooling strength worked well, and even when there wasn't much to go around, we stretched it between us like a two-way umbilical cord.

Don began chemotherapy treatments at a major teaching hospital in New York City. Two Friday mornings a month the children and I dropped him off at our local bus stop for his trip to the city. Don's parents, who lived in Connecticut, picked him up after each infusion and drove him home by Friday evening.

Lara was too young to understand, but four-year-old Marc needed some sort of explanation for the change in our lives. I told him that his father was going to a doctor in New York for special shots to keep him from getting sick, just as Marc and his sister had been given shots when they were babies. Not everyone needed Daddy's special shots. Marc didn't. Lara didn't. I didn't. But Daddy did. The shots would probably give Daddy a tummyache afterward.

Marc accepted my explanation with all the trust of an innocent child. I was half-ashamed of bamboozling him, but why mention cancer? Fortunately, the word didn't mean anything to Marc yet. If all went well, he would never need to know.

The chemotherapy treatments made Don violently ill. Worried that the kids would be scared when he vomited at home, he sequestered himself in our bedroom behind a door that only I was allowed to enter until he emerged, usually sometime Sunday afternoon.

Having to make our bedroom off-limits to the children was rough on all of us. Don had always been accessible to them. They didn't understand why they just couldn't burst in to say goodnight. If they did, Don would wake up and have to vomit.

Once, when Marc bounced unauthorized into our bedroom, I literally shoved him out the door. "Never again are you to open that door if it is closed," I hissed in an angry whisper. It crossed my mind that those were the words most panicked parents would say if they were caught by their children making love, not throwing up.

I tried to stay in the bedroom with Don, but sometimes I couldn't. Don's parents usually stayed over Friday night to help distract their grandchildren, but even then the children would call to me, needing some reassurance that their father was all right and everything would soon be normal again. If Don fell asleep, I sneaked out to be with them.

Don was weak from chemotherapy when we took our usual family vacation at my parents' lakeside cottage in Michigan that summer. He was too tired to join the sandcastle-making, but the children didn't mind that he just sat in a lawn chair on the dock watching us. He and Marc spent so much time fishing from the end of that dock that I began to think of their poles as extensions of their arms. They never caught anything big, and they always tossed the little ones back. A swan family visited the dock daily. Lara only got near the large hissing birds from the safe height of her father's arms.

After a year of chemotherapy treatments, the doctors recommended that Don have the remaining cancer surgically removed and we could no longer keep Don's cancer from our children. Lara, now two years old, only needed to be reassured that Daddy would return from the New York hospital as soon as he could. Marc, a five-year-old, needed more information. The idea that his father had to have an operation in the hospital to be healthy must have been confusing for him, especially because this time he would not be able to visit him there. His nursery school class had visited our local hospital, so Marc knew that some people need operations from time to time, though he didn't know about the effects of an operation on the body. When Don called him a few days after the surgery, Marc was puzzled by his father's voice. "What's the matter with Daddy?" he asked. "He didn't sound like he usually does."

"He's just tired and weak from his operation. He will feel stronger when he comes home from the hospital," I answered. I still hadn't tried to explain *cancer* to Marc.

The surgeon was unable to remove most of Don's cancer, because the tumor had invaded the major vein from his brain. Don's postoperative recovery progressed in spite of the bad news, and he came home to heal. There were small holes from drainage tubes in his chest which had to be dabbed with peroxide a couple of times a day to prevent infection. Lara made sure that I didn't forget my nursing duties. Every day she asked her father, "Where's your boo-boo, Daddy? Did Mommy fix it yet?"

When he was strong enough, Don started a second round of chemotherapy. I had thought the children probably took Don's treatments as a normal occurrence in their lives by then, but Marc was beginning to realize that his father was a special case. I don't think he resented his father's affliction, but he was grappling with understanding its intrusion into his relationship with Don.

One day when he saw the closed bedroom door again he protested, "I thought that Daddy was all through with his shots."

"So did I, Marc, and so did he, but he isn't. When Daddy was in the hospital, we found out that he needed more shots."

Later that day I took Marc and the little boy next door for a walk.

"My Daddy is sick in bed. He had a shot that gives him a tummyache," Marc confided to Chad.

"My Daddy isn't sick. He's mowing the lawn," Chad said.

Don, too, was beginning to grapple more and more with the consequences of his disease. After a consultation with another specialist who, for the first time, dropped the survival odds below fifty percent, Don cried. "I'm scared. I want to be your husband and Marc and Lara's father so badly."

"You will always be Marc and Lara's father," I said. "I promise you: you will always be their father, no matter what."

After only a few months Don's doctor decided that chemotherapy wasn't working well enough and that Don should have radiation therapy instead. We became occasional boarders with Don's parents, since they lived near a hospital with an excellent radiology department. Don was scheduled for a radiation treatment every weekday. Sometimes he stayed with his parents alone, leaving us at home so Marc could finish his last month of nursery school before summer vacation. Quite often the linear accelerator necessary for treatment broke down, giving Don a day off in the middle of the week. On those occasions he drove to New Jersey to spend a few hours at work, picked us up, and drove back to Connecticut, all in the same day. Marc didn't mind missing a day or two of school if he could be with his dad. We returned to our house every weekend just to keep the lawn mowed and the mail answered.

Although we wanted to make the time we spent in Don's boyhood home as pleasant as possible for our family, we never knew how much energy Don would have after each radiation treatment. Sometimes he and I just cuddled in his dark bedroom. Sometimes Don wanted to get right up and play soccer with Marc or take Lara on a walk to pick flowers. He wanted to enjoy the extra time he had with his children to the fullest. By acquainting them with the people and places of his childhood, he hoped to give them a knowledge of their heritage. They were so young to be building memories, but Don feared he might be running out of time to pass anything on.

In the woods across from his parents' home, Don showed us the tree in which he had carved his initials when he was a boy. Marc, an avid reader of *Ranger Rick* magazine, was scornful. "Daddy, Woodsy Owl wouldn't like that. It could kill the tree."

"Woodsy Owl wasn't hatched yet when I was a little boy, Marc." Who would have guessed that years later those carefully carved initials in that tree would represent a kind of immortality for Don.

Don helped Lara fill her bucket with wildflowers. Where the path divided we followed a hopping rabbit to the stream where Don wanted to show Marc how to catch frogs. The water was too shallow. The descendants of the frogs Don had caught in his youth had moved elsewhere.

Back at the house the kids showed Nana and Grandpa their buckets full of treasures: iridescent beetle wings, miniature pinecones, smooth pebbles, and bottle caps. The kids also found a butterfly lying stunned on the ground, barely able to flutter, a victim of a passing car. We carefully carried it home and placed it for protection in the flower box. We checked it periodically, but there was no change in its condition. The next day it had disappeared. The children and I asked ourselves whether it had died and decayed into the dirt or whether it had magically healed and flown away.

After a few walks on the same paths, we all felt the need to range a little farther away. One of our first excursions was dinner with Don's Aunt Steffa. The children were awed by the elegance of her antique-filled house so unlike the childproof practicality of their own home. When it was time to leave, I noticed that Don had perked up a bit after conversing with this vivacious lady in her eighties. They had always been fond of one another. I looked from one to the other and sadly wondered which one was nearer to the end of life.

We also took the kids to a nearby playground, armed with sand shovels and sieves. Lots of mothers, and an occasional father, pushed their tots on swings or held them on the seesaws. Don watched from a bench in the shade, tired from his therapy. Marc and Lara didn't mind. They liked to strike out on their own and made new friends with each visit.

One of our family drives took us past a cemetery. Marc was seldom interested in scenes passing by the car window, so I was startled when he asked, "What is a cemetery?"

I didn't want to answer; I was afraid it would upset Don, who was at the wheel. "It's where people are buried. You know that!" I said quickly.

"I knew, but I just wanted to hear it again," Marc said. Both father and son were struggling to understand death, Don facing his own and Marc struggling to understand the concept for the first time.

Later, alone with me, Marc wanted more information. "When someone is buried, if you want to see them again, can you dig them up and look at them?" he asked. I shook my head. "No," I answered.

"Why not? Is it against the law?"

"You just can't." I was reluctant to explain the changes wrought by death.

"What if you miss them?" he asked.

"Then you just have to look at their pictures and remember them in your mind or talk about them to someone else who knew them," I suggested. I had no idea that Marc would later remember and repeat those words to me during the initial shock of his grief.

I was glad that Marc had asked those questions of me and not Don. Answering the children's questions about the red lines on his body marking the radiation field was hard enough for Don. Those marks were not visible to strangers, but they couldn't be hidden from the children without changing our family intimacy. Lara often accompanied her daddy when he changed his clothes. One afternoon, Don told me, she broached the subject with an astute question. "Why do you have a window under your arm?" and Marc asked, "Why do you have paint on, Daddy?"

When Don's radiation treatments finally ended, we packed up and went home for good. Because his x-rays showed no evidence of cancer, we believed that we had beaten the odds. To celebrate his remission, Don and I took a Caribbean vacation while the children stayed with my parents in Michigan. After a week of pure relaxation, we jumped back into our busy family routine with a zest that pushed the shadow of Don's cancer to the back of our minds.

We showed off our carefully limited Caribbean tans to our friends at the pool club. Our kids splashed around with theirs in the kiddie pool. Marc finally enticed his father out of the shade by promising to show off his newly acquired swimming skills. Don stripped off his top and hurried to the pool. A little tan between the scars did make him look healthier, I thought.

With total confidence in his dad, Marc lost his usual fear of the water and jumped right into his father's open arms. Don took Marc paddling around the edge into the deep water. Don loved to swim, and for the first time, Marc seemed to love it, too. When it was Lara's turn for attention, Don sat on the edge of the kiddie pool and quacked for her rubber duckie.

We brought our friends home for a cookout. Don loved anything grilled over charcoal. He also loved the ritual of lighting and tending the fire and turning the sizzling food. The grown-ups had a few beers on the porch while the kids clamored all over the swing set. It felt wonderful to relax at home, enjoying the simple family pleasures so many people took for granted.

Don enthusiastically returned to work. Just before the recurrence of his cancer, Don had begun to receive recognition for his contributions to the field of evaluating teaching programs, especially those using computer-assisted instruction. He'd been promoted to a new position in his company, one combining his own research with planning for the direction of an important portion of the company's research. He was young to be entrusted with such responsibilities, but his brilliance in his field and his ability to work easily with his colleagues made him successful at what he did.

I was immensely proud of Don's accomplishments. I recognized him as someone special, not just to me but to the field of educational research. Unlike many of us, he had found the niche for which he was ideally suited in talent and temperament. He was respected and liked by his colleagues. His potential was limitless. It was no wonder that he kept his health problems to himself at work; it provided a refuge where he was not a cancer patient but a scientist. That his cancer had invaded his personal life was bad enough.

At the end of the summer we all returned to Connecticut for Don's checkup with the radiologist. Don's CAT scan was scheduled for a Friday afternoon. We spent the weekend with his parents waiting for the results. Finally Don decided on Sunday to take the children to the Peabody Museum to see the dinosaur skeletons. He brought his camera along, and before we went into the building he took pictures of the children on the museum lawn. "Those shots will turn out really well," he beamed.

Inside, he turned his camera on the dinosaurs and murals. Marc, fascinated by the prehistoric creatures, urged Don on. "Take the pterodactyl, Daddy, and the *Tyrannosaurus rex*." As I watched him snapping the shutter, I had no idea that by the time I'd get those snapshots developed, Don would be only a memory to us, like the memories he was trying to preserve in those photographs.

We were still waiting for test results on Monday, so we took the kids to the beach. Don loved the sea, not for sport, but for its creatures. In the water he caught a jellyfish in Marc's bucket. Marc screamed as Lara stuck her finger in the pail to poke it. "Don't touch it, it can sting you!" That settled that. The kids refused to go into the water any deeper than up to their ankles. But they waded and mushed around in the sand having a fine time; we tried to relax.

Finally the waiting was over and so was our brief respite of normal living. The results of the tests showed a new growth of Hodgkin's disease near the spot already treated in Don's chest. The radiologist prescribed another round of radiation therapy. Don decided to commute to his treatments by train rather than disrupt our family life any further by moving us in with his parents again. In order to catch the early train, he got up at four-thirty in the morning. He arrived back at our train station by mid-afternoon, just in time to put in a couple of hours of work before coming home to dinner.

After dinner he tried to spend a little time with Marc and

Lara, but sometimes he was too tired. When he had a little energy, the three of them climbed into our king-size bed and read books or watched the Muppets. Usually I tucked them all into bed at the same time and spent the rest of the evening alone, mindlessly staring at the television set.

By the time Don's radiation treatments ended in the fall, his cancer had spread to the other side of his chest. Radiation therapy was no longer an option for treatment, because there was a spot on his windpipe that appeared to have been adversely affected by the radiation. Experimental chemotherapy was started using a drug with much less severe side effects. In fact, on the day following a treatment, he usually felt tired but otherwise pretty well.

On one of these morning-afters Don decided that he was up to a family excursion. We took the kids to a farm near Don's office. It had an apple orchard, goats, sheep, and chickens and the children could feed them through a mesh wire fence. Don helped them toss in the corn without getting their fingers nipped. We loaded two bags of apples and a jug of cider into our station wagon and drove to Don's office.

The office complex, resembling a wealthy college campus, was set back on acres of land with handsome landscaping. We first trooped into the empty research building so that Don could open his mail while the kids stood on chairs to draw on his display board with colored markers. I looked around the room at all the family portraits and snapshots: pictures of Don holding each of his babies in the hospital after birth, pictures of Don and Marc shaving together and flying a kite, pictures of Lara and Marc in a box marked "Luvs." It was evident how much Don wanted his family near him, even at work. On his door was a picture that Marc had drawn. A circle of colored lines looked like thin flower petals without the center. Underneath, Marc's teacher had printed his title for him: "A bunch of snakes at a meeting."

We fetched our bag of leftover bread crusts from the car and wandered over to the company duck pond. Marc grabbed his share of stale bread and headed right for the edge of the water. I followed him to make sure that he didn't topple in. Lara was a little scared of the geese—some were nearly as big as she. Don stayed with her near the road, leaning against a reflector post for support. Lara bravely tossed the bread short of most of the ducks' reach. Don was unusually quiet and pensive.

When the bread was gone we piled back into our station wagon to head for home. In our driveway the kids darted out of the car and raced into the house to play. Their energy was inexhaustible. Usually Don followed close behind them, but that day he stopped still on our front walk. I nearly plowed into him because my arms were loaded with the bags of apples and cider, which he had become too weak to carry. I peeked around the bags, watching him. I worried that the outing might have been too much for him so soon after a chemotherapy treatment. Perhaps he needed to catch his breath. When I moved beside him, I saw that he was breathing normally, but he didn't seem aware of my presence. He was staring intently at our woods awash with fall colors. He neither frowned nor smiled. He was concentrating as if to memorize the colors of the last autumn he might ever see. I waited, still, beside him. After a moment he silently turned back to the beaten path into our house.

That evening he asked me, "What would you do if I died?"

"You won't, but if I ever needed to, I would go to Michigan near my parents," I answered.

Don nodded. "Your father would be good for Marc. The country is a good place for the kids to grow up. And they love the lake."

"Have you thought about where you'd want to be buried?" I forced myself to ask.

"No." Don began to cry softly. "I only want to be near you and the kids."

A few more weeks brought Halloween, our children's favorite holiday. Marc dressed up in a rhamphorhynchus costume. He smugly told anyone who would listen that a *rhamphorhynchus* was a flying dinosaur. The suit was authentic, right down to the bulb on the end of the long tail. Lara was Little Red Riding Hood, even though she screamed in fright at the thought of the Big Bad Wolf. I made both of the children's costumes as I always had done; they were the only clothes I sewed all year.

Don took them out trick-or-treating. The houses in our neighborhood were set mostly on grassy knolls above street level. Climbing up the driveways for treats required more energy than a kid got from eating each piece of candy. I knew that Lara would want to be carried, and I worried that Don would be too weak and in too much pain to manage. He still couldn't lift anything heavier than a pen with his right arm without feeling shooting pains from his incision. But the three\of them made the trek home, laden with goodies. Don had somehow carried Lara.

Three days after Halloween was our daughter's third birthday. Don came home from work early for her party. We played records of nursery folk songs for the children to dance to. Lara was wearing her party dress, and she plainly enjoyed being a girl. She held the hem of her skirt daintily in her hands while she tiptoed to the music. Don couldn't take his eyes off her. When he wasn't taking movies, he was gazing at her wistfully, perhaps wondering if he would live to watch her first dance recital, see her first prom, or dance with her at her wedding.

After the party, I left the playroom to start cleaning up cake crumbs in the kitchen. When I returned to check on everyone, Don and the children were standing stone still looking out through the sliding glass doors.

"Shh, Mom, look!" Marc whispered.

"It's a bunny rabbit, Mommy." Lara was too excited to contain herself.

"It's your birthday bunny, Lara," Don told her. "She came to your party to wish you a happy birthday."

Don had been troubled by a cough during his second round of radiation therapy, but it had cleared up by Marc's birthday, just two weeks after Lara's and a few days before Thanksgiving. Then over the holiday weekend, the living room filled with smoke because the fireplace damper had been closed prematurely, and Don's cough returned. Even after the irritating haze had cleared out of the house, Don's cough didn't cease.

With winter upon us, Don decided to wax my car in preparation for snow, salt, and sand. It was a job he had always done; he thought he could still do it. Unfortunately, he wasn't feeling strong. A troublesome virus had given him a runny nose, sapped his energy and worsened his cough. Like many chemotherapy patients he just didn't seem able to fight off infections. It took him four days of short work sessions to wax his way around my car, with Marc's help. He wouldn't give up. He couldn't reach the top because his arms were wasted from surgery and injections. He left little white streaks of unbuffed wax to mark where his reach ended; he planned to finish the job when he felt stronger.

A week before Christmas there were nine inches of snow on the ground. Our driveway had been promptly plowed so that Don could get his weekly blood test at our local hospital. Before he left, I bundled the kids up in snowsuits, boots and mittens for a romp outside. When I came back inside to get a carrot nose for the snowman we were building on the front lawn, I thought of inviting Don to watch us from the picture window, but he was talking on the telephone. In a little while, the kids and I tromped inside for hot cocoa. Don was staring out the living room window at the snowman.

"I came down to watch you, but you'd gone," he said wistfully.

"We were sledding around the side of the house," I said apologetically.

"I'm so jealous of you," he said without malice. "I wish I could play with them in the snow."

By Christmas his blood counts were too low to permit us to travel to Michigan, where we usually spent the holidays with my parents. So the children wouldn't be disappointed, Don insisted that we get a Christmas tree. We'd never had one before, because we were raising our children in the Jewish tradition of Don's family. Since we didn't have much to put on the tree, the kids and I baked gingerbread men and women to hang in plastic bags. I found three ornaments that had been given to me long ago and an angel that my mother had given to Lara for a keepsake when she was a baby. Marc had made a paper wreath in school with red, paste-covered berries. All we needed was the tree.

Only five days before Christmas, we braved the bitter cold and wind at the nearest Christmas tree lot and loaded a cumbersome bush in the station wagon. At home, Don struggled with the spruce to get the trunk into its brand new stand while the kids and I decorated the gingerbread people with frosting and cinnamon candies. Don stood our tree up in the dining room and collapsed into his favorite chair, wincing. He had strained a muscle in his weakened back dragging the tree into the house. He watched us decorate the tree from his chair. Our impromptu symbol of everlasting life was a work of art.

On an impulse I bought an electric train for Santa to leave us under the tree. Trying to sneak the gigantic box into our house, I made an unsuccessful sprint behind Don's back while he appeared to be intently watching television.

"What's that?" he asked, without even turning his head.

"Oh, nothing," I answered nonchalantly.

"That's too big for nothing. What is it?"

"It's a surprise for you and the kids," I replied.

"How do you know I'll like it? Come on, show it to me," he begged. Relenting I carried the box over to his chair and set it down on his lap. "I used to have a model steam train when I was a boy," he said grinning. "The kids will love a train."

Secretly I believed that the kids were really too young to be given a model train. They would need a lot of help when they played with it. But the train wasn't really a gift for them as much as it was for Don. I didn't know if there would be another Christmas for him when the kids *were* old enough. Don and the kids spent many delightful hours on the floor during that holiday, their heads bobbing in small ovals as they followed the movement of the train around and around.

Three days into the new year Don took Marc into his office for a visit. When they came back home, Marc excitedly showed me the gibberish typing that was his "work" from the office. He giggled as I read the nonsense out loud.

"Did you have a good time?" I really didn't need to ask.

"Yes, Daddy promised to do something special with me

every weekend, like we used to." I looked at Don for con-firmation.

"I've missed spending time alone with him lately. He needs the companionship," Don said.

Early in the week Don's parents arrived to babysit while I took Don to New York for a series of three chemotherapy treatments. I was supposed to attend a P.T.A. meeting the evening after the first treatment, but I was reluctant to leave Don with the children because he needed to save his strength for the two treatments that were left. He assured me that they would be fine for a few hours without me. He even looked forward to being in charge.

I tucked Marc into bed and left. Later Don's mother told me that Don had insisted on putting Lara to bed himself. If their interlude followed the usual routine, he changed her into her pajamas with a tickle or two, gave her a final drink of juice, and tucked her under her comforter with her worn, pink blanket. Don's mother heard him singing to his daughter, "Hush little baby, 'don't say a word. Papa's gonna buy you a mockingbird."

When I got home from the meeting just after nine-thirty, Don was waiting up for me alone. "I thought you'd be in bed," I said, pleasantly surprised.

"Not without you," he grinned. We nestled into the sofa together. I was amazed at his good mood on the night before a chemotherapy appointment. Usually he was nervous or de-pressed. I'll have to leave him in charge of the kids more often, I promised myself. We went to bed and made love tenderly.

After his final chemotherapy treatment of the week and a blood transfusion on the same day, Don slept in the back seat of the car while I drove home. He awoke as I pulled into a gas station on the outskirts of our town. I leafed through my near empty wallet. "Can I have a five, honey?"

"Sure." He dug out his wallet.

"I'd better go to the bank after I take you home. Do you need any money for the weekend?"

"No," he answered groggily.

"Won't you need some money for your special outing with Marc this weekend?" I reminded him.

"No," Don laughed, thinking of Marc's overflowing coin purse. "If I have to, I'll use his!"

"Where are you two going?" I asked.

"I told him we'd go to the pet store for some new tropical fish."

We pulled into the driveway and Don walked through our front door ahead of me. Lara flung herself into her father's arms. "Hi, Da-da!" she said, reverting to her babytalk endearment. They exchanged big hugs. Since the night that Don had tucked her into bed, the two of them acted as though they shared some wonderful secret.

Don and I went upstairs to our bedroom. We walked through the narrow spaces around our bed as Don took off his belt and I changed my shoes. We moved with the radar of time, gliding near each other but instinctively not colliding. That comfortable feeling of being able to navigate around another person had developed from years of living together.

I left Don stretched out on the couch as the children watched TV and his parents sat side by side on the loveseat quietly reading. "See you later," I called as I walked out the door to make the rounds of the bank, the grocery store, and McDonald's, but no one answered. Oh well, I thought, never mind. They're all engrossed in newspapers and television—I'll see them later.

While I was at the bank, Don got up from the couch to pour himself a soft drink. He lay back down on the couch watching his children watch television. Marc brought Don a slip of paper from his school bag.

"Look, Daddy, Amy gave me her phone number on the bus."

"That's nice. Do you know your phone number?"

"No."

"It's 555-3743."

"Can we call her?"

"Ask Mommy when she gets home, Tiger."

Marc went back to his television program. Don's mother thought that he might be hungry. "Don, there's some tuna in the refrigerator, if you want some."

"No, I'll wait for Linda." He had no way of knowing that his wait would stretch into eternity. He coughed, then rushing to the kitchen sink, he suffered a massive pulmonary hemorrhage, collapsing in his parents' arms.

On Friday, January 8, 1982, Donald Lewis Alderman, husband, father, son, friend, scientist, died of Hodgkin's disease at the age of thirty-five.

$\mathcal{T}$ELLING THE CHILDREN

$\mathcal{T}$he children were still watching television when I burst through the front door. Don's mother had called me at the supermarket where I'd abandoned two grapefruits and a bottle of club soda in my shopping cart to rush home. Five paramedics were bent over Don on the kitchen floor frantically preparing him for the trip to the hospital. As they carried Don through the living room on a stretcher and out the front door, the children faced the TV, but they peeked at the hurried departure out of the corners of their eyes. They were both silent as I made a hasty exit to follow the ambulance to the hospital. My only detour was to a neighbor's house to ask her to make peanut butter and jelly sandwiches for Marc and Lara.

The children, at home, endured the wait for news from the emergency room along with a sea of shocked relatives and friends. When I returned from my last look at my husband's sheet-shrouded body, my last stroke of his blood-stained hair, I immediately took my bewildered children by the hand and led them up to the stairs to the privacy of Marc's room, escaping the turmoil below.

I wondered if Marc and Lara would ever be able to love

me again after what I was about to say to them. The three of us, sitting silently on Marc's narrow bed with our feet folded beneath us, huddled together as if adrift in a life raft threatened by an approaching storm. With one deep breath I steeled myself to speak.

"I have something very sad to tell you," I began warily. I paused to give the children a chance to prepare themselves for the shock.

"I know. Daddy's dead," Marc blurted out. I should have realized that the children would know.

"Yes," I answered. "He was very sick. The doctors couldn't help him, and he died."

"Don't worry, Mommy. You can marry someone else," Marc said.

Momentarily shocked by this seeming disloyalty to his father, I understood Marc's desire to make his family whole again. I couldn't take away all of his hope. "Maybe someday, but not right away," I said.

Marc rushed on in a feeble attempt to stave off his emptiness. "But we can still remember him and look at pictures of him."

I agreed. "Yes, we will always remember him, but we can't ever see him again. He will never come home again."

Silence hung heavily as I tried to clear my numbed mind for what must come next. "Do you understand what *dead* means?" I tried to explain to the children in concrete terms something that even I could not yet comprehend. "Daddy can't move or breathe or see or think anymore. His heart stopped beating."

Marc remembered one of Don's favorite life functions. "Can he eat?"

"No." I almost laughed.

"Poor Daddy," Marc said with sympathy. His reeling mind produced a string of questions which I struggled to answer, as Lara sat in silence stroking her ever-present blanket for comfort.

"Will he turn to stone?"

"No."

"Will he get dirty?"

"No, we will bury him in a box to keep him clean."

"Will he be a ghost?" I cringed at the thought of the children being frightened by a haunting father. How could I offer them the comfort of his afterlife simply enough for them to grasp?

"His spirit will be with us," I ventured.

"What's a spirit?" Marc asked.

"Nothing that you can see or touch or hear. It's just a feeling of love all around us, the love that Daddy had for us."

"Is Nana going to die, too?" Marc asked. He had glimpsed Don's mother collapse on our living room couch in a state of shock before our hasty exit from the scene.

"No. She just fainted because she was sad."

"Will you die too, Mommy?" Marc's voice quivered. Lara reached out to nervously rub the loose skin on the back of my hand between her tiny thumb and forefinger.

"No, not for a very long time," I said with assurance.

"Then why did Daddy die? I hope I don't die," he pleaded.

"You won't. Once in a while someone gets sick and the doctors can't make them better. A tube inside Daddy that carried his blood broke. It doesn't happen very often," I assured him.

"How do you know it won't happen to me?" he challenged me.

"I just know." Some things have to be taken on faith.

"I miss Daddy," he sighed.

"So do I."

Lara had not yet spoken a word. Had she absorbed any of what Marc and I had been groping to articulate? I turned to hold her close. "Do you understand, Lara?"

"Yes," she said in her quiet, little-girl voice. "Daddy's gone."

After hugs I ushered the kids into my bedroom to watch the Muppets while I lay down on the bed to rest. I carried that off pretty well, I congratulated myself smugly. We had all taken it calmly. My family doctor had been right.

I'd called him from the hospital emergency room desperate for some advice. He had been straightforward. "The best thing is to tell your children directly. It's never as bad as you think it's going to be."

"Should I tell them when I get home or wait until tomorrow?" The kids still needed a good night's sleep, even if their father was dead.

"It won't get any easier," he'd said bluntly.

"If Marc breaks down in hysterics, will you come to our house?"

"Yes, but he won't," he'd assured me.

Telling the children had not been the shattering scene I had dreaded. Marc didn't fall to the floor crying hysterically. Lara didn't scream. In fact, they were cavorting around my bedroom imitating the Muppets when our family doctor, summoned to check on Don's mother, entered the room. He had been through so much with our family during Don's illness. Glancing at his animated young patients, he asked dubiously, "Did you tell them?"

"Yes."

"How did they take it?"

I gestured toward the two laughing imps and shrugged. "Just fine."

"They won't always be this happy," he predicted. "It will get worse, much worse, before it gets better."

"I'm surprised at how calm I feel," I confessed.

"Well, for the first time in a long time you're not in limbo. Some of the tension is gone now. You'll feel more later, after the shock wears off."

Again he was right. In my state of shock I was operating on automatic pilot. As responsible and loving parents, Don and I had put our children's needs ahead of our own. It was natural for me to continue that pattern when Don died. I felt little of my own pain immediately, too distressed about the suffering my children would endure because they'd lost their father's loving presence forever. Having lost one of the two greatest purposes in my life—being a good mate to someone I loved—the other purpose would keep me going. It was that commitment to Marc and Lara's physical and emotional well-being that forged what strength I was able to muster the night Don died and during the rough times afterward.

That night I had no clear-cut idea of what we faced or how to comfort my children. I knew that our first ordeal would be Don's funeral, and then we'd have to make many adjustments to our daily lives in order to continue to function as a family and to deal with our feelings of grief and loss.

Beyond that I expected only that the children's needs would become clear in their own time. Every child is different, and mine were no exception. I knew that because of their age difference Lara and Marc would have different questions and a different capacity for understanding what had happened to their father. Even so, I suspected that at some point they would show many of the same emotions of a grieving adult reacting to a major loss: shock and denial, anger and guilt, bargaining, depression, and finally acceptance.

How would I manage to guide them through this long grief process when I myself needed time and freedom from responsibility to grieve? I wanted to be strong enough to do everything possible for Marc and Lara; that was a way to continue to show my love for Don. This responsibility, this burden, was a test I dared not fail. We had entered a period of metamorphosis that I did not suspect would take years to complete and would forever change the course of our lives.

What I did know that night of Don's death was that the lives of these two children were all that was left of the man I loved. I was thankful that I had them, because without them I would want to die, too, rather than face the future alone. Even with them, the future looked bleak. We would not always remain calm in the days and weeks to come. Together we would grieve over our loss. My children had become mourning children.

The reactions of six-year-old Marc and three-year-old Lara on the night of their father's death were typical of children who experience the loss of a close, loving adult, especially a parent. They immediately looked to me, as their surviving parent, for the honesty and reassurance that would enable them to begin the work of mourning.

Because children's knowledge of the world is undeveloped, parents and educators strive to provide them with opportunities to learn at their own level of understanding. It is the same with their understanding of death. Just as children go through stages in their intellectual development, they also go through stages in their development of a concept of death. However, in our society children are given few opportunities to learn about the concrete aspects of death.

Marc and Lara had seen birds die from bashing their heads against our picture window. They had discovered crushed robin's eggs on our blacktop driveway and had even watched their father flush a few floating, motionless fish from his aquarium down the toilet. These typical childhood experiences reinforce the association between death and immobility that most children of Marc's age can comprehend. Children like Lara, however, may not have developed that connection yet. They typically associate death with separation, understanding that the dead are "gone." As difficult as it was for me to have to describe Don's stilled body, I knew that the details were important to help the children picture the reality of death, especially because they would not have the opportunity to actually see their father's body. When Marc wondered if his father would eat or turn to stone or get dirty, he was not merely indulging in morbid fascination. He was struggling to understand what death means in the same way that adults puzzle over the abstraction of life after death.

When Marc asked why his father died, he was asking how he died. If he had been killed in a car crash or in a fire, I would have told him. Illness as a cause of death is sometimes hard to convey to children because their knowledge of anatomy is scant and often erroneous. A heart attack or a "broken tube" happens inside the body and thus can't be observed. For young children, seeing makes believing easier. Later both children would ask that same question, "Why did Daddy die?" when they were really asking the reason for an accident of fate. At those times, I answered the only way I could: "I don't know why."

To soothe the children's fears that their whole world might collapse with the death of one parent, I needed to reassure them that I would not die. When Marc asked me if I would die, too, I could have answered with complete truth, "Yes, someday." Some experts say that is the only way to answer, because the children will not be so devastated if the surviving parent is run over on the street the next day. Yet the chances of that happening are so slim that I could not deny my children a sense of security. Besides, I asked myself, do you believe that you are going to die before old age sets in? No, I honestly did not. I knew it was possible, but I didn't believe it was probable. Why should I give my children a grim outlook which I do not accept myself? I don't believe that my answer was dishonest. Because a child's concept of time is so foreshortened, to answer "yes" would have led them to expect another crushing loss tomorrow or next week. "No, not for a very long time" was an answer that emphasized that their world would remain as secure as possible without a father, that they would not be completely without a protecting adult.

Marc wanted two parents and his immediate suggestion that I could remarry had nothing to do with a lack of feeling for his father. He was only expressing his desperate need to maintain the security that he was used to knowing.

And the depth of his love for his father showed in a fear that he might share Don's fate. Marc was of an age when his identification with his father was especially strong. They were alike, both boys, and they looked alike. When Marc asked, "How do you know it won't happen to me?," it was natural for him to think that they could die similarly, too. He needed to know that death at an early age doesn't happen very often, that though it had taken his father from him, he didn't need to fear his own death at age six. He had to realize that in death, each of us is alone.

There were also heartwarming moments in our conversation the night Don died. Marc's wish to remember his daddy and look at Don's pictures inspired many pleasant future interludes. Our family photo album, Don's personal possessions, and, of course, our separate and collective memories were to become important tools to ease our longing. Remembering the good times with Don would help us salve the sting of loss. Remembering together the funny times and even the grouchy ones, would help us feel less alone. Even being able to say to one another simply, "I miss Daddy," as Marc had done that night, helped us draw together as a family of three. We found a common bond that we did not have before. Blood is thicker than water, but grief is as thick and as hard as cement.

When I tucked the children into bed the night of their father's death, I told them that they could come to bed with me later if they felt too sad or lonely to sleep. I wanted them at least to start in their familiar beds so they could get some rest for the trying days ahead of us. Tired out by the romp in my bedroom and drained by the emotionally charged evening, they both settled down and fell asleep quickly. I sensed that Marc would have liked to fall asleep in my bed, but he had a special reason for wanting to spend the night in his own bed. He had lost his third baby tooth that morning. Before he went to bed, he tucked the little white kernel under his pillow, expecting the tooth fairy to come even if his father had just died.

Later that night as I plucked Marc's tooth from under his pillow, easing in a pack of sugarless gum and a quarter, I thought of how Don had enjoyed playing tooth fairy for Marc's first two lost teeth. As recently as that morning, he had smiled in anticipation of repeating his successful act. At least for this first important event without Don, Marc would not be aware of his father's absence. There would be many times in the future when Marc would long to have his father there.

With Marc's first lost tooth we had started a tradition of naming each one in commemoration. The first had been the "taffy tooth" in honor of the candy that had extracted it. The second had been his "Hanukkah tooth." We will have to stop naming his teeth, I thought regretfully as I wrapped the "Daddy died tooth" in a tissue and tossed it in the wastebasket.

I was glad to perform this little bit of fantasy for my son that night. As hard as it was not to have Don there, in accomplishing the little chore I felt a glimmer of my old strength come back. We could, indeed we must, survive. When there are children involved, life goes on immediately.

*T*HE FUNERAL

I could not sleep the night Don died. I paced my room, putting away his things. I scooped up his dirty underwear and tossed them into the hamper. I stashed his belt in one drawer and his comb in another. Then I found the manila envelope that the nurse had asked me to sign for at the hospital and emptied its contents onto the middle of our bed. His money, a few coins and bills, I stuffed into my wallet. His keys were tossed into the drawer with his comb. When the room was completely cleared of the illusion that he might be coming back, I crawled into my side of the bed. I lay there in a stupor, conscious of my breathing and heartbeat slowing down.

The rest of the house had finally quieted down. My own mother and father had caught a plane after I'd called them from the emergency room and were sleeping on the living room couch and loveseat. Don's parents had retreated to the guest room, but like me they hadn't found sleep easy. I had heard them stirring several times before I'd gone to bed, but they were finally still.

In my semiconscious state, I heard heavy familiar footsteps break the silence of the house. They trod up the stairs and down the hallway, stopping at the door to Marc's room, just a few feet short of our bedroom. They were Don's footsteps. I felt a moment of fleeting fright before the certainty that Don would never harm us settled my fears. I waited a few minutes for the footsteps to continue, but they didn't. I climbed out of bed and peeked through the partially open door into the hallway. It was empty. I checked on the children who both slept soundly. No one was in the bathroom either. Knowing that he had visited us, wondering if he ever would again, I slipped back into bed shivering at the eeriness of the night. Finally, I slept.

I awoke a few hours later feeling overwhelming fatigue. Bright sunlight streamed in the window. Why was the room so bright? Annoyed, I glanced at the window just long enough to see that the shade had not been pulled down. Why hadn't Don pulled down that shade last night as usual? Then I remembered. Don was dead.

I rolled over, dreading the sight of empty sheets where Don had slept beside me for the more than eleven years of our marriage. The sheets were not empty. Neither were they filled. Marc had taken his father's place sometime in the early morning hours. I crawled quietly out of bed to leave him peacefully, or at least deeply, sleeping. I could hear Lara babbling to herself in her room. I lifted her out of her railed bed and tiptoed downstairs with her in my arms.

People were stirring, making breakfast, talking quietly. As I stood on the stairwell looking over the hushed bustle that I knew would engulf me over the next few days, my knees slowly buckled. I sank into a squat on the steps, rocking Lara in my lap. I couldn't keep the pain at bay any longer and uncontrollable sobs bubbled up from my diaphragm. As I cried loudly, my mother let a spoon fall clattering into the kitchen sink and ran to take both Lara and me in her arms. She tried to soothe me with words, but I can't remember what she said, only of the tone of her familiar voice. Not wanting to scare Lara, I finally swallowed my cries and began crooning to her as my mother had just done for me. If I was this child's only remaining security, then she and her brother were mine. Their need for my love was the only sure thing left in my world.

Lara didn't notice anything strange about my tight, enveloping hug on the stairs. We had always been a physical family. As psychologists, Don and I knew that very young children who are deprived of touch can fail to thrive. To us hugging had been natural in times of joy or pain, and the children and I would hug more in the days and weeks to come. Our physical affection was good for me, a woman suddenly deprived of the touch of her spouse. Hugs were just as good for the children. My children had lost a great giver of nearly half of their hugs. Making up for that loss was one added responsibility that may have helped me get by as much as it comforted them.

I didn't sit on the stairs very long. I had to get us all packed to drive to Connecticut that very afternoon. Don's father had arranged his son's funeral; Don would be buried before sundown the next day, Sunday, according to Jewish tradition. The emergency room doctor had asked me to call them this morning to let them know who would pick up Don's body. He would be ready to be released to the mortuary this afternoon, after the autopsy I had authorized at the request of Don's oncologist, who wanted to find out the effects of the experimental drugs on Don's vital organs. I'd had no idea what to do about Don's body, so I'd been relieved when, after I'd gotten home from the hospital, Don's father had offered to handle the arrangements. He'd placed a hurried call to the funeral home that handled most of the funerals for members of their synagogue. The funeral home would handle everything.

There was very little discussion about what kind of funeral we should have. Don's parents must have talked about it in the night, but they were reluctant to broach the subject with me. Sometime Saturday morning his mother approached me, saying only that they would prefer to have a simple graveside service, if that was all right with me. I didn't really care, so I agreed. None of our friends or Don's co-workers could get to Connecticut on such short notice, but the funeral would be for Don's parents and other relatives, who might as well have it the way they wanted.

No one talked to me much that morning, not even the children. Everyone seemed to be waiting for some kind of cue from me. They must have sensed that I didn't want us to wail and moan together. They all knew me, knew that I needed to withdraw in times of stress and be alone, at least for long enough to muster the will to share what I felt. Except for a few questions about what to do during these next days, they left me alone. Grandparents played with grandchildren as they usually did, helping me but also preserving a little longer the feeling that everything was as it used to be. Immediately after breakfast, which nobody ate, Don's parents left for home to begin preparations.

Getting our clothes packed for the trip meant getting Don's packed, too. I was selecting one suit of clothes without shoes, with not even the change of underwear that I was used to packing for Don's business trips, when Marc walked into the room. He watched me fold the shirt I had bought Don for our trip to the Caribbean and stuff it into the garment bag along with a Father's Day tie.

"Who will dress Daddy?" he asked.

"There are special people called undertakers who get dead people ready to be buried. They will dress Daddy and put him in his box," I explained. Marc seemed relieved that that particular distasteful task would not fall to his obviously exhausted mother.

Marc watched silently as I continued packing. I tried to think of something constructive and comforting for him to do on his own. He seemed so aimless. "Why don't you and Lara go draw a picture that we could bury with Daddy in his box. Then he would always have something with him that you gave to him. You know, sort of a good-bye present."

"Okay." Marc went off, I assumed to follow my suggestion. The children were somewhat subdued, and they, too, seemed to be waiting for directions from me about what their part would be in an unfamiliar and grown-up ritual.

As soon as we could throw ourselves together, we climbed into the car with my parents for the three-hour drive to Connecticut. In that day's stormy weather it took almost six hours. I hadn't had the presence of mind to listen to a weather report, and the warm sunshine of New Jersey gave way to pelting snow in New England. I hadn't even packed the children's boots or snowpants.

When we reached Don's parents' house late that afternoon, crowds of people were already milling about. Even the nine people who would be staying there constituted a mob. Don's father must have been busy on the telephone from the time they had arrived back home. Relatives drifted in and out. Some brought food, adding to the dishes that Don's mother was hastily preparing. The children and I were in a fog, mine induced by the shock, theirs induced by the confusion. My parents, also at a loss in unfamiliar surroundings, occupied themselves by caring for the children.

We ate some of the condolence food for dinner, and then Don's father and my father took me to the funeral home to pick out a casket. In his office, the funeral director spoke to us briefly about plots and prayers. Then he led us down to a basement full of caskets. The cheapest one looked too small for Don. I couldn't imagine him scrunched up inside it. I quickly chose another whose finish reminded me of the pine furniture that Don had ordered specially made for us.

It had been twenty-four hours since Don died, so the funeral director recommended against viewing Don's body. State law forbade viewing without embalming, anyway, and embalming was a practice that was against Jewish tradition.

I would have liked to give the children the chance to see their father's body. The concrete experience of seeing him in his casket might have helped them accept the reality of his death and to understand what was being done with his body. I was relieved, though, not to have to face that ordeal with my children so soon. If the funeral had been a few days off, I might have had the time to prepare myself and the children for a family viewing that would have been a positive experience. It could have been a time for the three of us to share our good-byes and to talk more about death and loss. As it was, I was too exhausted to think or feel anymore. All I wanted to do was to get back to Don's parents' house and sleep.

When we did return, there were still too many people around for me to settle down. I tucked the children in bed, and they didn't protest. They, too, were exhausted from the strangeness of the day. I was a little worried about their too-normal behavior. They'd been entertained by their usual games and stories during the harrowing car ride, and they'd settled down to play with my parents as soon as we'd arrived in Connecticut. They hadn't even protested when I'd left them to go to the mortuary. Like most children, the onset of their mourning was not immediate. They were still being well cared for by my parents and I was still nearby, so they were fairly content.

I wanted nothing more than to sleep like my children, but relatives continued to straggle in. Don's sister and her husband came in from California. His cousin, Ron, from Florida, was the last to arrive. After we hugged and cried a little he joined some of the men who sat in the den with the television droning beneath their voices. The women sat in the formal living room. I stood, trying to make an exit to go to bed. I nodded in agreement to words that I didn't really hear. My ears were attuned to the bedroom down the hall where my children slept and where I wanted to be. Then I heard Don's voice as though it came from amidst the men in the den saying, "It's all right, Hon." My eyes widened in shock. It had to have been Don. No one else called me Hon. I quickly excused myself and slipped down the hallway to the door of the den. Ron was talking. Everyone in the family said that he and Don looked and sounded alike. I shook my head. It must have been Ron's voice I heard, the words muffled on the way to my ears. I continued down the hallway to rest with my children.

We slept together in one room that night and the next. Marc and I shared the bed and Lara curled into an old crib. The nights of closeness were good for us. Behind the closed bedroom door, we took comfort in the peaceful feeling of our three living bodies breathing together. Although some experts warn that allowing bereaved children to sleep with their surviving parent may lead to a dependency that is unhealthy for both parent and child, I didn't give our sleeping arrangements a second thought. I was sure that no pattern was being set that would have to be broken later.

On the morning of the funeral I awoke despondent. The knowledge that Don would be buried in a few hours pierced through my foggy state. Lara tossed in her crib. Marc and I cuddled for a few minutes. Then I opened the door to send Marc to the bathroom, but I collapsed back on the bed. For a second day I cried loud morning tears. My father came from the open door of his room to hold me. "It hurts so much, Dad," I told him.

"I know," he said. I quieted quickly, seeking consolation by tending to my children. Marc didn't seem to be disturbed by my tears, perhaps because they didn't last any longer than his when he hurt himself in a fall. He may also have been taking stock of what was happening around him. Children usually take longer than adults to show their grief, because their first concern is whether they will still be taken care of as they were before the death. To reassure my children, I nudged them both down to the kitchen for breakfast.

Although there were still a few hours before the funeral, people would soon be descending upon us again, so after breakfast I dressed the children together. Marc was pouting as I handed him his clothes. "Do I have to go?" he whined. "I don't want to see them open the box."

"They won't open Daddy's box," I answered, realizing suddenly that the children had no inkling of what we adults had hastily planned for Don's funeral. Never having attended a funeral before, Marc and Lara did not know that caskets are never open for Jewish funerals. We adults had agreed that Don's service should be a simple graveside farewell. Hadn't the children overheard our brief planning? I couldn't really remember. Once I had been told that the mortician had completed the arrangements, I had pushed the impending ceremony out of my mind, relieved. Everyone who needed to know the details had been informed. Everyone except my children. After we'd dressed in the warmest clothes we had brought with us, I sat the children down and briefly explained what to expect at their father's funeral.

"We will go to the cemetery just to say good-bye to Daddy. The rabbi will read a poem and say a prayer."

I talked a little about the hole in the ground where they would bury Daddy's box. I told the children that Daddy's box would be near the hole, but that they didn't have to worry about falling into the hole when they said good-bye. There would be chairs for us to sit on beside Daddy's box during the poem and prayer. If they knew what the place would look like and what the service would be like, they would feel more comfortable.

"Okay," Marc said. "I'll go." He looked down at his legs. "I don't like these pants. They make me sad." They were his grown-up dress slacks "just like Daddy's." Marc had worn them for our family portrait taken less than three months earlier.

"Do they remind you of Daddy?" I asked just to acknowledge his feelings.

"Yes," he admitted. The three of us quickly finished dressing.

I did not for one minute consider leaving the children at home during their father's funeral although well-meaning friends and relatives questioned my wisdom and even my sanity. I did not want the children to feel deserted or left out, nor did I want them to wonder if the funeral was something horrible they were not allowed to see. In general, the funeral service helps children to accept the finality of death. By seeing adults grieving, children are reassured that their own feelings of grief are normal which frees them to cope with their feelings openly and constructively. Attending a funeral can also prevent frightening fantasies about the dead person. Erna Furman says in her book, *A Child's Parent Dies,* "[Experts] stress how hard it is for children to recognize and accept death when they are deprived of the opportunity to participate in the funeral rites and visits to the cemetery, which confirm the concrete aspects of death, or when they remain uninformed or misinformed about the death."[1]

I also believed that giving children the choice of going or not going to their parent's funeral, as some advise, makes sense only for older children. Marc and Lara were not old enough to carry the burden of that choice, I thought. It was too big a decision for them to make under the stress of Don's death. What if there are regrets later? As an adult, he or she may wish

[1] Erna Furman, *A Child's Parent Dies* (New Haven: Yale University Press, 1974), p. 246.

the childhood choice had been different, may even feel guilty about the decision not to go to the funeral.

If the surviving parent wants a child to go to the funeral, I do not think that parent should ignore his or her own wishes. If it were necessary, I would have said to my children, "I'd like you to go to your father's funeral because you are a part of this family. I'd like you to be there with me."

Most children prefer to stick close to their surviving parent anyway. If a child expresses reluctance to attend the parent's funeral, that reticence may stem from fears about what will happen or how he or she will react, in the way that Marc feared viewing his father's body in an open casket. Taking the time to ask why the child doesn't want to go can ease the child's fears. If we had planned an open casket viewing at Don's funeral, I would have accommodated Marc's wishes by keeping him a safe distance from the open casket or by having him arrive after the casket was closed. The needs of the immediate family should dictate funeral arrangements, and no one is more immediate than a bereaved child.

Some children, especially little boys, are afraid of crying in public. Well-meaning relatives or friends may even have told them that "brave men don't cry." Well, big boys do cry, especially at their fathers' funerals. I wish that I had told both my children that everyone at Daddy's funeral would be sad and that lots of us would cry. That I would cry. And that it was perfectly all right for them to cry, too, if they felt like it. In the same way that happiness is more fun when we share it, sadness hurts less when we share that, too. I didn't tell them that, but I think they sensed it from the way Don and I had always shared in their childhood sorrows ranging from scraped knees to broken toys.

As soon as we were dressed, relatives began to return to the house. I dreaded greeting them and listening to awkward condolences again, but steeled myself to face the company anyway. The children instinctively stayed away from the crowd of strangers. One of Don's thoughtful cousins brought them some of her daughter's toys and Marc and Lara played quietly in the bedroom with my parents for company. By mid-morning the cumulative effect of all the sympathy finally peaked beyond my endurance, and I retreated to the bedroom to join my children.

I didn't come out until Melissa and Danny arrived from Massachusetts. They had been our close friends before they moved from New Jersey two and a half years earlier. We had met them while sprawled on the floor doing panting exercises in Lamaze classes preparing for the births of our sons. Marc was two weeks older than their boy, Jason, and their daughter, Magan, was a month older than Lara. For Don's funeral they had left their children home.

I burst into tears when we hugged just inside the front door. They greeted Marc, who had followed me out of the bedroom, and apologized to me for arriving later than they had planned. Icy roads had delayed them, and there wasn't any time to talk before we had to head for our cars. I was grateful when Melissa volunteered to sit in the car with my children at the cemetery if Marc and Lara couldn't stand the bitter cold, though my mother had already offered to shepherd her grandchildren during the funeral.

That arrangement would be a big help to my children. Marc knew Melissa from the many times she had watched over his play with Jason and he trusted her friendship. Marc felt completely comfortable with her. Lara and her grandmother were, of course, familiar cookie-making and story-reading buddies.

Having a warm, dependable adult "assigned" to each of my children during the funeral, just in case I wasn't able to give them support, was a tremendous relief to me. Like my son, I too was uncertain how I would act at the funeral. What if I fainted in the dirt at the cemetery? My children would be upset. My clothes would be soiled. What if I cried hysterically? Would my children then become hysterical, too? Knowing that someone would be there to soothe and comfort each of them no matter how I acted made me less anxious. Relaxing a little gave me the control and confidence to face the trip to my husband's open grave calmly.

Even though emergency caretakers were assigned to Marc and Lara, I really wanted to be the one to draw my children close in comfort. For a child whose parent has died, no one can substitute for the surviving parent. If I could support and reassure them from the very beginning, I could lessen my children's anxiety that they might no longer be safe and secure with just me. It would also ease my own doubts that I might not be able to carry the load alone. After all that I had been through already, I could do it now. Just in case, my father was watching over me.

As I bundled Marc and Lara into their winter jackets, I explained to them that they might have to miss part of the funeral. If they got too cold, Melissa and Grandma would take them back to the shelter of the warm car. Then my parents, my children, and I scurried through the chilly front yard into my car for the drive to the cemetery. As we pulled out of the peaceful dead-end street, Marc looked troubled. "I don't have anything to give Daddy," he said with disappointment. "I didn't have time to draw a picture."

I had forgotten all about my suggestion to him the day before when we were hurriedly packing. It seemed so long ago. I kicked myself for not following through. I didn't want Marc to feel that there was something more he should have done for his father, and I had felt that Marc would be comforted knowing that something he had made with his two little hands would stay close to his father forever. Why hadn't I taken the time to find that orange-juice-can pencil holder that Marc had made Don last Father's Day? It was too late now. Don's casket had already been sealed.

I tried to make amends as best I could for letting Marc down. "I put Daddy's I.D. bracelet in the box with him from all of us," I told him. Although Don had worn no jewelry except his watch and wedding band, we'd given him the gold-chained nameplate last Hanukkah. I had wanted his name buried with him in a last-ditch effort to immortalize the man. "It says, 'Love, Linda, Marc, and Lara' on the back," I reminded Marc. "The flowers on his box are from us all, too."

Marc seemed satisfied. "Will they bury the flowers with him?" he asked hopefully.

I didn't really know. "Yes, I think so."

I know other families who have found solace in adding

family treasures or gifts to the dead parents' graves. One friend, Nancy, who had her husband's body cremated, told me the lovely story of the burial of his ashes several months later when the ground had thawed. "We all wrote him a letter, even my four-year-old son. His older brother and sister helped him. None of us wanted to read them out loud. They were our personal good-byes, things we wanted him to know. We all cried, though, and each one of us dropped our letter into the ground with his ashes. I'm glad we did that." I envied Nancy the time that she had to prepare her family both emotionally and practically to say a memorable good-bye.

When we stepped out of the car at the cemetery, the wind chill factor made the air feel like it was ten degrees below zero. As I hustled the children past the hearse toward the wrought-iron cemetery gate, the funeral director slipped me an ordinary bulging white envelope. I traced the circle of the bulge with my thumb and forefinger. It was Don's wedding band. I was glad we were burying his bracelet with him to signify our marriage and our children. Planning to save his ring for Marc, I slipped the envelope into my pocket and proceeded through the gates with the children, hand in hand.

We sat down in the row of metal folding chairs for only a minute. Someone said, "Linda, it's too cold for the children." In truth, it was too cold for any living thing. With regret I realized that Marc and Lara couldn't stay for even part of the service. I would have to come up with a quick good-bye gesture spontaneously, something significant enough to suffice as a "funeral" for the children. I pulled them toward me and spoke softly to them to make the moment more intimate.

"I am sorry, but it is too cold for you two to stay out here and listen to the poems and prayers. I'll tell you about them later. Grandma and Melissa will take you back to the car where it is warm. I'll be there in a few minutes. Let's say good-bye to Daddy now. Aren't the flowers pretty?" I rose up with a child on either hand, uncertain what to do next.

My father stood, too, leading Marc the two steps to Don's polished pine coffin. Dad touched his fingertips to his lips and then gently pressed a kiss to the smooth wood. "Kiss your father good-bye," he suggested. Tears filled my eyes at the beauty of the gesture, and I repeated the kiss. "Good-bye, Don."

Lara, too, willingly imitated her grandfather and mother. "Good-bye, Daddy."

Marc alone hesitated.

"Don't you want to give Daddy a good-bye kiss?" I asked. He shook his head. "Okay. You don't have to. Go ahead with Melissa and Grandma. I'll come soon. Give me a hug." I embraced each of the children and passed their two small hands over to my father.

As my father squeezed Marc's hand, he turned back and tried one last time to urge Marc gently to face the concrete evidence of his father's death. Dad stroked the coffin again and whispered to Marc, "Would you just like to touch it?" Marc, wanting to please his already substitute father figure, gingerly patted the corner of the coffin and sighed. "Good-bye, Daddy," he said softly. Then he dropped his grandfather's hand and led the way through the rows of gray tombstones to the line of parked cars.

As the rabbi started chanting, my body began to shiver. Someone behind me said, "Move in closer to shield her from the cold." I smiled crookedly. Didn't they know that I was not shivering from the cold, but from the terror of facing the rest of my life alone, separated from my husband forever by six feet of solid dirt? As the others bowed their heads in prayer, my tear-stained face mystically rose heavenward as if an unseen hand were lifting up my sagging chin. I stared into the snow-clouded sky until everyone else had said their private good-byes and my father and I were left mercifully alone.

I stood slowly and moved close to Don's coffin. "I love you, Don," I sobbed. "And I promise you," my voice rose to a fevered pitch, "I promise you that the children will never, ever forget you! Never!"

"He knows that," my father gently reassured me, taking my elbow to lead me away.

Hurrying back to the warm car, we narrowed to single file on the packed dirt path to let two grubby-looking men with shovels pass in the opposite direction. Crass, I thought. But I couldn't really blame them for not waiting the extra few seconds for me to get clear of the cemetery. The cold was so painfully sharp.

I quickly climbed into the back seat of the car to see how my children were faring. Marc was calmly talking to Melissa about what Jason had been up to lately. Lara was in the front seat alternately sobbing and screaming, "I want to say good-bye to Daddy. I want him to be out of his case!"

My mother passed her over the seat to me and I held her on my lap. "It's all right, Lara," I said. "You did say good-bye to Daddy, but he couldn't come out of his case. He can't ever come out of his case again." Lara cried her dirge all the way back to the house.

Thinking Lara had heard me tell Marc that Don's casket would not be open, I had expected her to understand that that was how she would say good-bye to her father at the cemetery. I should have realized that she expected to say good-bye as she always had, physically, with a hug and a kiss. I should have taken the time to sit down and have a longer talk with my children, both when Marc's question came up as we were getting dressed that morning and just before we left for the funeral. I should have told them more than once exactly what would happen at the cemetery and what they would be doing to participate. I should have asked them if they had any more questions. I should have asked them if they understood. I should not have made so many mistakes. And Don, you should *never* have died.

ADJUSTING OUR LIVES TO OUR LOSS

The morning after Don's funeral the children and I returned with my parents to New Jersey. Marc and Lara needed familiar surroundings and so did I. Most experts agree that young children express their grief more freely when they feel personally safe and secure and when they know they will be loved and cared for as they were before their loss. Keeping them away from their familiar routine and surroundings would only compound their loss and increase their insecurity. Their toys, beds, and friends are all important to their healing. Though Don's parents wanted us to stay for the traditional mourning period, I couldn't face that, especially knowing my children needed to be at home. I, too, needed to begin the slow, tedious task of reordering our lives.

On the drive home my mother told me that she would be glad to stay with us as long as we needed her. My father could stay only five or six more days because he had to go back to work. I didn't even have to think before accepting their offer. There would be advantages and drawbacks to having my mother stay with us, but they could help me in settling the business of Don's death. It would be less of a hassle if I didn't have to take the kids along with me. And with someone to screen visitors and phone calls, the sympathizers would intrude less on my time and especially on my much needed rest.

On the other hand, although I dreaded being alone because I would miss Don, I also longed to relax the stolid manner I had maintained for the two years since the recurrence of Don's cancer. In short, I needed to unwind, to be human. It was really my fault that I let my mother's presence inhibit my expression of grief; she would gladly comfort me. But I hated to have her hurting for me, so I often kept up the facade that all was well.

Everything back home looked just the way it had always looked. It didn't seem like a house shrouded in tragedy. With the rest of the mourners and the casket back in Connecticut, the reality of Don's death was in another, faraway place, not here.

I was in a daze of knowing but not feeling and immediately jumped into doing what had to be done for our daily life to continue as smoothly as possible. I felt as if I were in a race with myself to get the "things" done before the emotions hit and incapacitated me.

Marc wanted to know if he could go back to school, so I called his kindergarten teacher. A friend had already informed her, but I wanted her to expect Marc's return the following day. I didn't see any purpose in making him stay home just for the sake of propriety. He needed to return to his normal routine as quickly as possible. His teacher, a warm woman, said she would welcome him back, but added that she had decided not to inform Marc's classmates; she'd leave that up to their parents. I wondered how she expected those parents to learn that a father of their children's classmate had died. Her silence might mean a lot of shocked kindergarteners if Marc decided to "show and tell" that he had spent the weekend at his father's funeral. I was too tired to discuss my doubts on the phone with her that night, though. She had always been a good teacher, so I left up to her the question of how to handle her small pupils.

The next afternoon, Marc seemed perfectly happy to be going back to school, even though it meant leaving Lara home with her grandparents to get all of the attention. I began to think about what would be good for Lara after her grand-parents left. With some misgivings, I concluded that the best course was to start Lara in nursery school two mornings a week as soon as we were settled into our new routine.

The first school experience is a monumental change for a child, and Lara was special, a newly bereaved three-year-old. I worried that adjusting to school might be too much of a stress when she was simultaneously coping with the death of her father. As with Marc, I wanted to keep her surroundings as familiar as possible to nurture her sense of security.

But I also knew my own limitations. I would desperately need those two mornings a week as respite from my new twenty-four-hour-a-day job of single parenthood. There was no one with whom to share the joys or the burdens any more. No one to whom I could say, "Watch the kids, honey, I'm running out for a loaf of bread." No one to ask, "Will you please take the kids outside to play while I get dinner? It's been a miserable day." I would need time alone just to manage the everyday tasks of our daily lives and to mourn.

I hoped that Lara, too, would benefit from time away from me to develop a new independence. She was a gentle, loving child, but shy, as I had been as a youngster. I had always secretly enjoyed the exclusive attachment to me she so often showed. "She's a mama's girl," I'd boasted more than once. Now things had changed. She no longer had her father to dilute the intensity of that attachment to me. If she coped with her loss by constantly clinging to me, I might eventually become resentful of her. I also didn't want to inhibit her progress into childhood by building a closed little world that neither of us would ever want to leave. I couldn't live through her, nor she for me alone.

Mid-year openings in nursery schools in our town could be scarce, but I was lucky. I called the director of my favorite local nursery school. The appropriate class was full, but the teachers agreed to add Lara under the circumstances and be-cause they needed girls to balance the class. Lara was to start school on the first of February, just in time for Valentine's Day.

I knew I could trust Lara's first teachers to take good care of her emotional wounds, since I had observed these teachers working with the children a few years back, when I was looking for a nursery school for Marc. Lara's new teachers were affectionate with their charges, good substitutes for a warm and physically demonstrative mother.

My mother helped dispel the guilt I felt about the sudden arrangements, admonishing me not to be too hard on myself. I realized, too, that dealing with our new situation would take more time, energy, and levelheadedness than an overworked parent could muster.

My parents were also concerned that I might have trouble adequately supporting our family, so they nudged me to call the social security office immediately and to find Don's life insurance policies. As distasteful as those jobs were, I did them because one of my highest priorities was to continue to fulfill my children's basic needs with as little disruption as possible.

The death of a parent leaves one person to provide for the bereaved child, a person whose judgment may be clouded by his or her own grief. Studies have shown that the death of a spouse causes more stress than any other major life change. Unfortunately, many young widows and widowers rush into decisions that not only add to their stress, but also affect how safe and secure their mourning children feel.

I was very fortunate that Don left me financially secure enough; no immediate change in our lifestyle was necessary. Oh, I went through the typical widow money panic, all right. In the first few weeks I wasn't even sure where the money to pay the gas bill would come from, since half of the amount in our joint bank accounts was frozen until Don's will could be probated. I was thankful Don had paid the mortgage two days before he died. I relaxed a little when the social security checks started coming earlier than I had expected and the life insurance was safely invested in my local bank. Though it took me several months, I realized that we could live about as comfortably as we had when Don was the breadwinner of our family. By then I was also glad that I had not made any decisions immediately after Don's funeral that would have disrupted our lives unnecessarily.

I had read Lynn Caine's excellent book *Widow,* in which she urgently advises readers not to make any important decisions during the mourning process. I agreed with her instinctively. If I were to go to work or sell our house, the two biggest decisions a young widow often rushes into, perhaps to avoid loneliness and the anguishing memories of a spouse's presence, it would have added to my stress as well as to the children's insecurity. Although I already knew that I would eventually want to move, probably back to Michigan to be near my parents, now was not the right time. Neither could I go to work and leave Marc and Lara. One of their parents had left, and one loss was enough. Someday I would want and need to go to work, but now my children needed me.

For the courageous widow who, for financial reasons, has to go to work or sell her house, I have only admiration. Those changes, however, do not have to be insurmountable problems. Moving to a more affordable house within the same school district or the same neighborhood when possible means the children don't have to adjust to a new school and new friends. If a move farther away is necessary, relocating near relatives or friends is a good idea. They can provide some support and companionship until everyone has a chance to make new friends. Even a place merely familiar to the family, like a favorite vacation spot where the memories of good times linger, gives the whole family a more positive attitude about having to leave.

If going to work is necessary, there are things to do to minimize the grieving child's additional loss. A job that allows the surviving parent to spend time with the children will make both parent and child much happier.

Good child care is essential. For the young child, a day care center with trained, professional staff is one option. If the child has friends already in day care, he or she will be happier still. Another option is care by a familiar relative, friend, or neighbor. Some of these people might even be willing to come into the home to babysit. Some companies today even provide day care at the job so parents can spend lunch hours and breaks with their children.

Sometimes older children may not want to come home from school to an empty house after the death of their parent. In that case, arrangements can be made for someone to be there or for them to go to a neighbor's or friend's house after school.

For a family with the room and financial means, a housekeeper is one choice. If there is a college nearby, a student might trade housekeeping duties for room and board, though adjusting to a stranger may not be easy. Bereaved parents must ask themselves how much a part of the family they want the helper to be. It may be best to make the bereaved family's need for privacy clear in the beginning.

Widowers, too, are often confronted immediately with the need to find good child care. Some have recommended against using the term *widower* when advertising for a house-keeper. This avoids attracting someone who wants to fix everything for the poor widower and his poor children, especially if the fixing includes remarriage. Applicants can be informed of the details of the family's circumstances in an interview.

Children take any necessary change better if the surviving parent has a positive attitude, though this is not an easy task for a grieving, fatigued parent. It may help to remember that children heal better when they feel secure and trust their parents to care for them. There is no reason to feel guilty about having to make changes in order to satisfy their basic needs. When there is no choice, we must do what has to be done. In the long run, the changes may benefit both parents and children: parents often grow stronger from the success of balancing a career and still providing for the needs of a family, while children can become more self-confident as they take more responsibility for themselves, their home, and even their siblings. Whatever else changes, the love between parent and child which makes the sacrifice bearable must remain stable.

Filling Marc and Lara's need for my love and affection was as important as filling their basic physical needs. Nothing makes a child feel more insecure than the loss of love, and my children had lost their father's ongoing love. Because I was now their only major source of love and support, I knew that it was crucial for us to continue the avenue of communication that Don and I had fostered with them from infancy.

Equally important was the need to establish communication about their father's death and the general concept of death so that they could feel more comfortable with what had happened to us all. One mistake is to avoid conversation about death with bereaved children because they don't understand death on an adult level. Instead, adults need to talk on a level that children *can* understand. Ignoring a death only increases the bereaved child's fear that something is horribly wrong—wrong enough to be unspeakable—and forces them to bottle up their feeling of loss. Unless they have the opportunity to express their emotions, the effects of unresolved grief may haunt them all of their lives.

Death is not an easy topic for most parents to discuss with their children. It is especially difficult for the surviving parent sorting through her or his own feelings of grief and loss. I was no exception. I turned for help to the county children's librarian, Miss Rohrbacher, who had been reading stories to my children from the time they were two years old. When I called her she was genuinely saddened by the children's loss. She would be glad, she said, to get together any books that might help Marc and Lara understand what death meant and cope with their father's death.

Identification with a book's characters can comfort bereaved children by informing them that they are not alone in their loss and that they are not abnormal simply because none of their friends' parents have died. A book on the subject may bring out the emotions of grief—anger and sadness—that have not previously surfaced. Often it is less painful to think or talk about a book character's loss than to confront one's own loss. This is because the character's loss is at a safe distance. Once a child's grief is expressed in empathy with an imaginary character, parents can help their children recognize and accept their grief. Finally, sharing books with young children helps them learn the words to express what they're feeling.

Reading to our children had been a favorite pastime for Don and me. Using children's books to stimulate and supplement our question-filled conversations was natural for us, so I was confident that Marc and Lara would not be put off by whatever books Miss Rohrbacher could find for us.

I knew that I would need all the resources I could muster to help my children understand even the simplest facts of death. The day after we arrived home from Connecticut, Lara's questions told me that explaining the mysteries of death only once to a young child is not enough. With Marc loaded onto the midday school bus, I picked up Lara and carried her upstairs for a nap. Her mind was on her daddy.

"What means 'dead'?" she asked. "Can he talk?"

"No." I shook my head.

"Can he move?" she wondered.

"No, his heart stopped beating."

She thought for a moment before searching through the mound of stuffed toys in her railed youthbed. "Where's my lamby and teddy?" she asked anxiously. The once-treasured gifts from her father had long ago been put away with her other infant toys. I was amazed that she remembered them. Slightly troubled by her regression to a more secure time, I rummaged through her cupboard until I found the two missing animals. I tucked in the three of them, Lara, Lamby and Teddy, all snuggled together.

After unpacking our clothes from our trip, I rested and waited for Marc to come home from school. He ran cheerfully into the house as usual, ready to watch his favorite cartoon, "Scooby-doo." I asked him how things had gone at school and he answered with a perfunctory "Fine."

Had anyone said anything about his absence yesterday because his father died? "No." That was it. I didn't press the point. I just brought him a snack and let him settle into his beanbag chair in front of the television set.

When I took the children to the library for story hour later that week, I picked up the books that Miss Rohrbacher had searched out for me. As she handed over the stack of slim books, she apologized. "I couldn't find a single book for young children about the death of a parent either in our catalogue or in the list of books in print. There just aren't any." She pointed to the books in my arms. "Those are about grandparents or pets. Maybe they will be of some use." She shook her head. "I just couldn't believe it!"

I could. While the children were occupied with story hour I took the opportunity to check the adult shelves on the topic of parental death. There was only one book, Erna Furman's *A Child's Parent Dies.* Two others were for older children. Both would have started a dialogue between the two mourning generations, but both were too advanced to share with my children.

The books that Miss Rohrbacher ferreted out were still immensely helpful to the children. I read to the children from the time we got home from the library until we had to quit and eat the dinner my parents had prepared. For several days we read those books over and over again. Lara's favorite was *The Dead Bird.* As a three-year-old, she was struggling to grasp the immobility of the dead, a concept that usually develops by age five. The book clearly and simply explained to her the physical changes wrought by death. Having missed so much of her father's funeral, she took an avid interest in the children's funeral for the bird. At the end of the book, the children place some flowers on the dead bird's grave and leave to play. That separation from the dead was the one concept of death that she was able to understand.

Marc, more sophisticated at age six, took to *When People Die,* a book every bereaved child should own, as should every elementary school library. With beautiful pictures and beautiful words, it told Marc why people die, what happens to a person in death, both in body and spirit, and how people feel when someone they love dies. The book's emphasis on the naturalness of death helped us all in our overwhelming sadness at the unnaturally premature death of our father and husband.

I left the books on the shelf where we always kept the children's library books, so they could have access to them any time they wanted. Sometimes they asked their grandparents to read to them, and my parents welcomed the opportunity. Sometimes Marc or Lara curled up alone with a book to "read." Though they couldn't yet read the words, even looking at them alone was helpful, because in private children may drop the need to hide their grief. When the books were due back at the library, I ordered copies of their favorites from the local bookstore.

Although it was important to communicate with Marc and Lara about their father's death, I didn't want it to overwhelm our memories of the abundant love he had already given them, the strongest link we had to Don. Marc's consoling response the night I told the children that their father was dead ("But we can still remember Daddy") and my assurance that we would always remember him inspired me to invent a new bedtime ritual, "Remember Daddy Time," two weeks after Don died.

After brushing our teeth the three of us would perch on one bed, and instead of reading a book, would tell one of our favorite memories to each other. After the first few times, we didn't do it every night. The children were eager to participate because it was fun and like sharing a secret. There was no pressure, and if one child didn't want to remember, they could just sit and listen. Usually if I started talking, long-forgotten memories would pop into our heads. If Marc or Lara asked to be first, I deferred. By sharing, each of us collected three times as many precious memories as we had separately.

Marc remembered the time that he and Daddy had won a plastic trophy at the Flemington Fair, another time when he and Don had gone fishing and come back without so much as a minnow, and the time that he and Daddy had built three snow forts in the yard in one day. I didn't remember the last. It must have been some storm.

Lara, the thumb sucker, had a lot of oral memories. She recalled the many times that Don bought them candies from the machines at his office when she and Marc visited, the days when we were in Connecticut for radiation therapy and all sang boisterously while playing "ring around the rosy" on Don's parents' front lawn, and the time we fed the remnants of hotdog buns to the seagulls at the ocean shore.

I told the children about things they could not possibly remember. There was the summer of 1976, during Marc's infancy, when Don and I bought our baby a print of a little tousle-haired boy soaring in the snail-shell basket of a hot-air balloon. There was the time in the last month of my first pregnancy when Don and I lay side by side on our bed, absorbed in the Marc Chagall lithograph on our wall. "Let's name him Marc," we decided. There were the Sunday afternoon walks we used to take over the Lambertville–New Hope bridge to Pennsylvania for milk-and-honey ice cream cones. Don wheeled Lara's stroller while I held Marc's shirt as the toddler dangled over the bridge to watch the mighty Delaware River flow below.

Memories . . . we still share them, even though Remember Daddy Time has gradually faded away as our lives have become more crowded with soccer games and piano practice. Yet in the weeks following Don's death, the simple ritual came to possess the significance and serenity of evening vespers for us.

Although meeting the children's needs was my first priority, I had needs of my own that I could not neglect without endangering my ability to function as a parent.

The list of things that had to be done to settle Don's estate seemed endless. In addition to filing for social security benefits and life insurance claims, both of which required copies of Don's death certificate, I had to have Don's will probated, register the cars in my name, change all joint financial and credit card accounts, apply for new health insurance, change my will, name guardians for the children, and file inheritance taxes. I had to decide what to do with Don's retirement annuity, find a financial adviser, designate Don's memorial fund, inform faraway friends of Don's death, and phone the local papers with Don's obituary for starters. If my mother hadn't been there to watch over the children while I slowly accomplished all of these tasks, I would have been in a frenzy.

Her presence also gave me something essential to my well-being: time to mourn without the distraction of my children. Just as they would have suffered from unresolved grief throughout their lives had they not expressed their feelings, so would I have.

Two weeks after Don died, his colleagues held a memorial service for him at his office. I decided not to bring the children, because the speeches would be over their heads and because it might confuse them to have a second "funeral," especially without any concrete evidence of Don's body. Moreover, I wanted to do something that would be a comfort just for me. I welcomed the service as a time to receive the sympathy and support of Don's co-workers, many of whom were also friends from the time I had worked in the same office before

Marc's birth. Among these people I felt complete freedom to share my personal burden of Don's loss for the first time.

The service gave me a chance to plan a more personal tribute to Don than the hasty funeral. I chose one of Don's favorite pieces of music, Respighi's "Pines of Rome," to be played as people settled into the crowded room. A biblical quote from the *Song of Songs* that had been read at our wedding adorned the cover of the program and a dozen long-stemmed red roses decorated the table next to the speaker's podium. I placed our family portrait in the front of a guestbook signed by most of the mourners, including the president of the company. I arranged to have the speeches recorded so that the children could listen to them when they were old enough to understand. Perhaps the speakers knew that, because all addressed at least part of their speeches to Marc and Lara, though I did not. I delivered the final eulogy, reminding the staff of Don's guiding belief that the research they conducted had importance only as a tool for improving the quality of people's education. People were what counted to Don, not just proving his theories or methods.

After the service a woman I didn't know approached me. "Your speech was the one that really captured the essence of the man," she said. "He treated everyone, no matter who they were or what they did, like a king."

I also treasured the condolence cards and notes from Don's co-workers that poured in for weeks after his death. Every afternoon I walked to the mailbox with anticipation. Then I allowed myself the luxury of curling up in a corner of the couch, alone, to wallow in the sympathy each envelope contained. "We are so sorry . . ." "What a terrible shame . . ." Occasionally one of the children would notice me open a brightly flowered card that looked suspiciously like a birthday card and ask, hoping for a piece of cake, "What is that for?"

"Oh, it's just a card that so-and-so sent to say how sorry he is that Daddy died," I'd briefly explain before stuffing it into a bulging box for safekeeping. Those cards were so important to me. I still remember my panic and dejection the first day that I opened the mailbox to find not a single card or letter there. Perhaps if I had shared the cards with them, Marc and Lara would have been comforted to know how many people had loved their father and were shocked and grieved by his death.

Someday I must open that tucked-away box and let Marc and Lara explore all those messages. The day will come when their curiosity about Don and their need to become reacquainted with him will motivate them to ask. Knowing how much other people respected Don might help them form an image of him as a man as well as a father.

On one of those trips to fetch a delivery of sympathy cards I ran into a neighbor who asked me how I was doing.

"I'm tired," I said.

"You ought to take an exercise class," she advised. "It would do you good."

I laughed for the first time in days. "An exercise class! I hardly have the energy to walk to the mailbox," I told her.

Although exercise might have been good for me, the one thing that I did begin to do for myself was to write a journal of my own emotional journey and the progress of my children's grief. I also wrote the story of the last two years of Don's life and his fight to live. Someday the children would want to know how he died, and I didn't want to remember all the details until they were old enough to understand them. I had to go on living, too. So I used whatever time I could find to satisfy my compulsion to write, eventually arranging for either a relative or a baby-sitter to care for the children once a week. With great subterfuge I kissed the children good-bye, walked out the front door, circled around the house, and sneaked in the back door and down the basement steps. I prepared my retreat with bananas and a hot pot for brewing tea. I didn't tell anyone, because it all sounds a little bit crazy. Maybe it was, but it helped me get by. It satisfied my need both to vent my emotions of grief and to do something that I had always enjoyed doing just for myself.

Other widows and widowers have chosen different ways to meet their personal needs during the early period of bereavement. Those who have the energy and the spare time when they won't be missed by their children might want to get a part-time job or volunteer for a few hours a week. Both activities can satisfy the longing to be with other adults. Some seek the solace and companionship of a religious organization. Many widows or widowers have already established club memberships or hobbies that can be sources of support. Gardening seems to be a favorite hobby, perhaps because nurturing life is an antidote to death.

None of these choices was right for me during my early bereavement, because I was too busy, too tired, and too occupied with my children. Later I did all of those things, and even took an exercise class. But at first, I wrote. Since that time I have given blank books to a few newly widowed friends suggesting that writing it out might help.

It might have been easier on both my children and me if I had taken more time for self-nurturing than I did. Instead of trying to do it all myself, I should have used more of the help that my friends and relatives offered in all those sympathy calls. Later I learned that accepting help was no reflection on my ability to be a good single parent. It was, in fact, what my Jewish relatives call a mitzvah. Allowing people to help gives them the opportunity to do something concrete to express their grief and empathy.

Many widows and widowers are needlessly reluctant to seek professional help, too. One of the most reassuring pieces of advice out of the many I received during those early weeks of mourning came from a counselor. He was the speaker at the next P.T.A. meeting I attended after Don died. After his speech I approached him and bluntly asked, "Is there anything I can do that will prevent the death of my husband from having a terrible effect on my children in the future?"

He answered me kindly, "If they ever have any problems, you will be there for them, won't you?"

"Of course!"

"Just let them know that," he finished.

That small piece of advice would center me in the weeks and months after Don's death. As my children struggled to understand death and express their grief, I tried, no matter what other mistakes I made, to be there for them.

UNDERSTANDING CHILDREN'S CONCEPT OF DEATH

"Daddy can't move," Lara commented one day shortly after Don's death. Then an exciting idea struck her. "Peter Cottontail can drag my Daddy back!" It was a good idea—rabbits live in holes in the ground and, now, so did her father.

"No, he can't, Lara," I corrected. "Daddy has to stay in his case. He can't ever come back."

"It's not good to bury Daddy in the ground," she protested. Immediately she revised her idea into one she thought more plausible. "Peter Cottontail can bring him some cough drops." Don had sucked constantly on cough drops during the final days of his illness.

In *A Child's Parent Dies,* Erna Furman explains the young child's need to communicate with her or his surviving parent about the facts and fears of death. "With the youngest children the task of supporting their mourning includes helping them to understand the concrete aspects of death, furthering their grasp of the specific circumstances and cause of the parent's death, helping them to master their anxiety in connection with it, and assisting them in differentiating themselves appropriately from the deceased."[1]

From Lara's comments about Peter Cottontail and her father's body, I realized that she had a lot of work to do to understand the concrete aspects of death and their effect on her father. I would need to help her understand death just as much as I needed to encourage the expression of her grief so that her progress through the mourning process would not be impaired. The same would be true for Marc even though he was older. His numerous questions told me that he, too, needed honest answers in order to develop a more complete and mature understanding of death. Though adults experience shock, anger, and sadness in response to a loved one's death, they often protect their children from the facts of death. Lacking an understanding of the nature and extent of their loss these children remain in a state of confusion which is far more stressful than the normal progression through the phases of mourning.

Psychologists who have studied childhood perceptions of death have concluded that children's level of understanding about death is related to their level of cognitive development. Children gradually build an accurate and mature understanding of death as their thinking ability advances throughout childhood. The child psychologist Jean Piaget found that children move through four cognitive stages as they grow from infancy to adolescence.

According to Piaget, babies from birth to about two years of age are in the sensorimotor stage of cognitive development, in which sensory stimulation and motor activity gradually become the basis for their thoughts about their environment. Because babies have only the germinating seeds of language and thought, they have no conception of death. By the age of six months, however, they do have a strong attachment to both of their parents and to other significant people such as siblings or grandparents. John Bowlby found that babies who are deprived of their mothers suffer in a predictable

---

[1] Erna Furman, *A Child's Parent Dies* (New Haven: Yale University Press, 1974), p. 114.

way. First, they protest her absence by crying and throwing temper tantrums, all the while expecting her to return and soothe them. Next, they fall into despair, becoming inactive and withdrawn. Finally, they detach themselves from the mother and turn to others to care for them. If the mother does come back, they may reject her.

When a baby's parent dies, the continued care and attention from the surviving parent becomes vitally important. Young children who are deprived of a warm, dependable substitute caretaker may never achieve a healthy detachment from their dead parent, remaining instead in continuous despair.

Even though babies have no concept of death, surviving parents and other caretakers need to be prepared to guide bereaved youngsters as they grow older and begin to develop an understanding of their loss.

Between the ages of about two and seven, children are in Piaget's preoperational stage. Young children in this stage are egocentric, assuming that other animate and inanimate things have thoughts, feelings and abilities just like their own, a fact well known to the makers of children's cartoons. This egocentrism leads children to believe in the power of their wishes, and they indulge in magical thinking, in which they believe they can control events with their minds. These children are also learning to use symbolic language to think and talk about the past, present, and future, which allows them some comprehension of age, space, and time. Although happenings can now be viewed sequentially, these children have not yet developed the ability to integrate a sequence of events into an overall view, so their concepts of age, space, and time are often inaccurate. They tend to concentrate on one aspect of a situation and ignore others, which leads to illogical thinking. Focusing on one single event and then jumping to another, the preoperational child often generates incorrect cause and effect conclusions.

Early in this stage children can comprehend death only as a separation, similar to Daddy's absence on a business trip or Mommy's stay in the hospital to have another baby. Like the sensorimotor babies, they believe that the dead parent will come back, and thus they may react in the same way as a baby.

Eventually, as their thinking and language progresses, preoperational children begin to comprehend death, but in a very immature way. They have not grasped the idea of time as a continuum rather than as an inconsistent series of events, so they do not understand that death is permanent. Fairy tales and cartoons reinforce the idea that death is not permanent. Snow White ate a poisonous apple, but the prince revived her with a kiss. Countless cartoon characters are regularly blown up or knocked out, only to immediately return intact to the television screen. But to say that fairy tales and cartoons cause children to believe that death is not permanent would be to make the mistake in logic of the preoperational child.

Because these children's egocentric thinking directs them to rely on their own experiences to learn, they also believe that their dead parent continues to function in the grave the same way they remember the parent functioning in life. Children at this age typically envision the dead parent still eating, sleeping, and thinking. They may even attribute to that parent feelings of love and loneliness, the very emotions that they themselves are feeling.

If they are uninformed about the cause of a parent's death, they may make their own erroneous conclusions and develop irrational fears. It is not uncommon for a child of this age to be afraid of hospitals or ambulances because they preceded the parent's death. The child reasons, "Mommy went to the hospital, and then she died. If I go to the hospital, I will die, too."

By around age five, most children have come to identify immobility as the outstanding characteristic of death. They have witnessed spiders and ants become motionless under the pressure of their own tiny shoes. They will play dead by stretching out rigid on the ground. Even a prodding playmate may only be able to make them flop from one motionless pose to another. But at the end of the game their death is always reversible. They come alive to play another day.

From the ages of about six to eleven, children become less egocentric in their thought as they progress through Piaget's concrete operational stage. They can consider several aspects rather than focusing on one when drawing inferences, which allows for more accurate conclusions about the physical facts of the world, including death. During this stage children master some universal concepts about the properties of their world. One of those is reversibility, which is the knowledge that an operation can be reversed to bring certain things back to their original state. For example, a cup of water that has been poured into a glass can be poured back into a measuring cup and will be the same as it was before it was poured. Children who have developed the concept of reversibility can also begin to comprehend what is not reversible and to deal with the concept of finality, which is the end result of irreversibility. By practicing and mastering these concepts, concrete operational children learn that certain rules are applicable to whole classes of physical matter in the world (all liquids can be poured back, i.e. reversed). Armed with this knowledge and the ability to generalize by taking several recurrences of an event into account, children come to understand universality. By the age of eight or nine, they begin to play games with very definite rules that must be followed universally by all players. What happens to one should and does happen to all.

Reversibility and finality are important to understanding that death is indeed irreversible and permanent. When these concepts are mastered, children can accept that their dead parent is never coming back. Thus, children in the concrete operational stage may have deep emotional reactions of sadness and depression upon the death of a parent.

Universality implies that death will happen to all of us someday. Knowing by this stage that death will someday happen to them, children around the age of eight sometimes develop a strong fear of death, both their own and of other loved ones who might die and leave them alone.

Despite their fears, children at this age are intensely curious about death, and the surviving parent may find the child consumed with questions that are distasteful to answer. These children are finally catching on to what death is. They want to know more, which seems to be their attitude toward the world in general.

As developed as children's cognitive skills become, they

still are not able to deal very effectively with abstract ideas until approximately above the age of eleven, when they enter Piaget's formal operational stage. The adolescent has the ability to look at things from several angles to solve problems in many ways. Adolescents can conceive of numerous possibilities at once. Because they have the ability to think abstractly, they have a fairly mature, well-developed concept of death as a normal part of the life cycle. But as any parent of a teenager knows, the adolescent seems to regress to the level of a four-year-old when it comes to egocentrism. Unlike the young child, the teenager's egocentrism is not rooted in an immature ability to think. It is more of a social egocentrism, a preoccupation with the importance of self in relation to the rest of the world. For this reason the teenager is almost as susceptible as the child to thinking that their parent's death may be their punishment for some bad behavior or argument with the dead parent, even though the teenager knows the actual cause of death was an accident or illness.

I could recognize from my children's questions and comments during the months following Don's death that they were in different developmental stages and that their concepts of death were appropriate to their different chronological ages. Three-year-old Lara, in the beginning of the preoperational stage of cognitive development, understood that death meant separation from her father, but couldn't fully grasp both his immobility and the permanency of his death until two years later, when she progressed to the brink of the concrete operational stage.

Marc, a bright six-year-old when his father died, was beginning the concrete operational stage of development, and, after my first explanation of his father's death, never questioned the immobility of death nor the permanency of his loss. He accepted death as final, but he was full of questions about the physical aspects of death. However unpleasant his questions were to me, I answered them honestly. Children in this stage still learn through their experiences, and Marc needed his questions answered in order to reach a more accurate understanding of death. Most of the time he did not seem upset by my descriptions of the details of death. Instead he was curious.

It was much more frustrating for me to try to communicate with Lara on her level of understanding and be honest at the same time. So often I was tempted to lie just to avoid hurting her with the truth. I kept telling myself that lying would only hurt her more in the long run, but I still felt like a mean mother.

Three weeks after Don's death Lara and I had lunch alone while Marc was off at school. My mother, who had been handling most of the household chores on top of caring for her grandchildren when I was busy, had finally worn out and was taking a nap. Lara took advantage of our privacy to talk.

"Daddy's never, ever coming back," she stated without much conviction.

"No. But he didn't want to leave you," I answered.

Lara's statement was so tentative that it seemed more of a question than an expression of her own belief—as if she were trying out something she'd heard me say but hadn't yet adopted as her own conviction. I thought it was best to give her the confirmation she seemed to be seeking, but also to provide some consolation.

Later in the day she tried out the idea again. "Daddy's warm in his box, but he's never, ever coming back."

I didn't try to correct her erroneous assumption that Don could still feel hot and cold because it was a normal thought for her age. Besides, permanency was enough for her to grapple with at one time. "No, he's not," I agreed.

At dinner she raised the point for the third time. "Daddy's never coming back."

"No," I repeated.

"Can Daddy come back?" she asked genuinely.

"No."

"Why?" she demanded.

Trying to answer simply enough to make her understand, I was direct. "He's dead. He can't move."

"Daddy didn't want to leave us, yes?"

"No, he didn't." At least she needn't feel rejected by her beloved father.

"Poor Daddy!" she said with pity.

When I asked myself why it was so difficult for a child of Lara's age to accept that a dead person never comes back, I had to admit that, given her belief that dead people still possess life functions, the idea that a dead person would come back is perfectly logical. If Daddy can move, he would choose to come back as he always had when he was away before. The only thing I could do to help Lara understand that death was not the same as a separation was to reinforce continually the fact that her father was not coming back and to give her time to mature enough to understand that fact.

Young children who are grieving over the separation from a dead person sometimes have a hard time coping with separations from others who are close to them. Only a month after her father's death, Lara had to be told that her favorite storyteller was taking another job and moving to Seattle. Lara's reaction was immediate. "Miss Rohrbacher will never come back to the library again," she lamented. Separation and death were linked in her mind. Moving away was as permanent as death.

Miss Rohrbacher did come back to visit story hour several months after she left, but by then Lara had detached from her and seemed unaffected by seeing her again. I even sensed a slight rejection in Lara's cool manner toward Miss Rohrbacher. But that experience alone did not clarify the difference between separation and death for Lara.

For six weeks after she started nursery school in February, Lara balked at our parting each schoolday morning. On her first day of school I stayed with her and watched her hesitantly join in the class activities. After that, however, on the two mornings a week of school, she cried when I left her. Her distress when she left me was even worse than I had anticipated. Each time I heard her being carried off sobbing while I hightailed it out the door, I felt wretched. When I had taught nursery school, I had always advised mothers to leave their crying children with me, because once Mom is out of sight, tears dry up quickly. Now that I had to leave my own daughter crying, I was less sure of that advice. I was comforted to know that one or the other of Lara's teachers rocked her in the big oak rocking chair every day until her tears ceased. The rest of the morning, I was told, she played quite happily. Eventually her crying time grew shorter and finally it stopped altogether.

Adjusting to the temporary separations of preschool did not immediately change Lara's connection between death and separation. She was simply too young to think any differently. And her immature concept of death seemed to cause her frustration when confronted with the reality of her situation. Not only couldn't she comprehend that her father's death was permanent, but because she could not understand that death brought immobility and the cessation of all other life functions, she wanted her absent father to continue to have feelings, too.

One afternoon when Marc, Lara and I were playing companionably in our living room Lara asked in her usual manner, "Do you love me?"

"Yes, I love you very much!" I answered in my usual manner.

"Does Daddy love me?" she asked as though defying me to answer negatively.

Somewhat intimidated by my three-year-old daughter, I answered, "Yes, he did love you when he was here." I emphasized the "did."

Lara was outraged by my change of verb tense. She screamed incoherently.

Marc tensely observed his sister's tantrum from across the room. Unable to tolerate her pain, he tried the old diversion tactic. "Look at this, Lara!" He tempted her with one of his toys that he usually forbade her to touch. Instantly she stopped yelling and rushed to grab the bait. Perhaps I could have calmed her better if I'd reassured her that she still had her father's love in a spiritual sense, that his love would be with us forever, but children of Lara's age are as likely to be confused as comforted by such explanations during their struggle to understand the permanence of death. This just was not the right time for that type of consolation.

Several times after Don died Lara showed me that it takes a great deal of patience to deal with a child who was still in a beginning stage of comprehending death. I came to see that seven times is not enough to answer the same question for a bereaved child. Seven times seven may not even be enough. Just when I thought that Lara had finally begun to understand because she had stopped asking if Don could come back, she threw me a curve.

"When Daddy is alive again . . ." she began.

I couldn't stand hearing that one more time. I cut her off. "Daddy won't ever be alive again," I stated firmly.

"Maybe he will," she answered haughtily.

"No, he won't." I sighed.

When she continually used the present tense—"Daddy does this" or "Daddy does that"—I didn't know whether it was only a lapse of grammar or whether it meant that she still didn't grasp the permanency of his death. Each time I patiently corrected her with, "Yes, he used to do this or that."

Finally one day she corrected herself. "Daddy lets me shave with him." She smiled as she remembered the lost morning ritual. Still smiling she rephrased her remark. "Daddy *used to* let me shave."

I hoped that moment was a step closer for her, which would help alleviate some of her frustration at not being able to understand the immobility and finality of death. Even so, I expected to be answering her repeated questions on both of these aspects of death for some time. I knew that she had a lot of growing and questioning to do before she understood as Marc did. He knew that death meant immobility, and he knew that his father was not coming back because death was irreversible. His concerns were different from his sister's, tending more to the physical and social aspects of death.

One morning Marc and I went for a walk around our neighborhood, pulling Lara down the street in their little red wagon. Perhaps the confinement of the wagon reminded Lara of her father's coffin.

"Daddy's in his case," she remarked casually. "He died."

"Yes," I agreed. "Because he died, he had to be put in a case and buried. It's called a coffin."

"Why are some people put in a coffin when they die and some people aren't?" Marc wondered.

"People in different parts of the world do things differently." I shrugged.

"Was Daddy wrapped up in bandages?" Marc wondered.

"No, he was buried in some of his clothes. We don't wrap people up any more," I said.

"They only did that in ancient times?" he asked.

"Yes," I answered, amazed that his concept of time included "ancient." He used to think that his grandparents were ancient.

Marc's questions about death customs here and now as well as in other countries and times may have been part of his attempt to begin to understand the universality of the concept. He was beginning to see that death happens to everyone even though different cultures handle it in different ways. He was also intensely curious about what "our way" was.

Someone had belatedly sent me an extra copy of Don's obituary and Marc spotted the clipping on my desk.

"There's Daddy's picture from the newspaper," he pointed. "Are his eyes open?" Marc bent over for a closer look.

"Yes." Why did he ask that, I wondered.

"How did they get his eyes open?" he puzzled.

Finally I understood. "That picture was taken a long time ago when Daddy was alive. Newspapers don't take pictures of dead people," I assured him somewhat inaccurately. I had always thought that our society's prurient interest in pictures of bloody, twisted bodies on the newscasts and in newspapers and magazines was a sign of a national character fault. However, Marc's many ghoulish questions made me realize that part of our fascination with these pictures may be our attempt to comprehend the concrete aspects of death in a society that stunts the normal understanding of death by removing our experiences of death as far from us as possible.

To facilitate Marc's development of a mature concept of death I had to answer his questions even when they were distasteful to me. The paradox of children about Marc's age is that their questions, which may continue for years, seem so cold to many adults. Yet once these children can comprehend the finality of death, their emotions run deep. Although Lara was more vocal in her protests about her father's death in the early weeks, Marc's despair was just as great. Like many adults, he just didn't always show it. Facing mortality is terrifying, and it is sometimes safer not to look.

Yet as Erna Furman pointed out, as well as understanding the concrete aspects, children need to master their anxiety about death for healthy mourning to proceed. One of the most troubling aspects of children's reaction for surviving parents to witness is their own children's fear of death. Although many four- and five-year-olds fear the death of people they love, their egocentrism usually protects them from fear of their own death. Older children's fear that they will die typically peaks around age eight or nine when they grasp universality.

Yet very soon after their father died both Marc and Lara expressed fears that they or people they loved would die. Perhaps their fears were greater than those of other children their age because the experience of death was so close to them. They had lost the protective security of their father, so that no death, not theirs or mine, seemed out of the question.

One night the three of us were driving in our darkened car on the way to the movies as a special treat. We usually went to matinees, but on the spur of the moment I decided that it would be good for us to do something together that had been fun for us before Don died.

"I like riding in the car at night," Marc hummed. "It's so cozy."

"So do I," I agreed.

Suddenly Marc sighed. "I wish I could do it with Daddy."

"So do I. But we still have each other." I tried to maintain the snug mood.

"Why did Daddy's tube break?" he asked again.

"Because he had something growing inside him that wore the tube down and broke it," I explained once again.

"How do you know it won't happen to me?" he asked, challenging me.

"Because it doesn't happen very often, only once in a while," I said.

"Does it ever happen to women?"

I sensed that he was beating around the bush. "Yes, but it won't happen to me," I reassured him. "It rarely happens."

"Only once in a family?"

"Not even once in every family. It doesn't happen at all in some families." I tried to control the resentment in my voice.

"Then why did it happen to Daddy?"

"I don't know." Honestly, I didn't.

Even Lara was worried that what happened to Daddy could happen to her or to me. One afternoon as I took away her empty apple juice cup and tucked her tightly into her bed for a nap in her favorite position, on her tummy, she observed, "My heart's beating."

"That's good. That means you're healthy," I diagnosed.

She flopped over onto her back to kiss me "goodnight." "My heart stopped beating," she panicked. "The juice made it stop."

"No, it didn't. It's still beating," I reassured her. "Drinking juice can't make it stop."

"What if it stops?" she challenged me.

"It won't," I repeated.

Apparently Lara wasn't fully convinced, because not too long afterward I had to soothe her fears again. Missing Don at bedtime, that quiet, tradition filled time of day, Lara softly chanted as I tucked her in, "Daddy's never, ever coming back."

"No," I agreed.

"Maybe his heart will start beating again," she fantasized.

"No, it can't. He's dead."

"I want to go in his case and cuddle with him," she pleaded. He had always cuddled her at bedtime.

"You can't. His case is buried in the ground," I reminded her.

"He won't ever come back?" she asked.

"No."

"He will never pick me up?" She was on the verge of tiny tears.

"No." So was I.

"They won't put me in the case?" She seemed suddenly fearful.

"No, they won't put you in a case," I promised.

"I won't die?" she asked in a panic.

"No, not for a very, very, very long time," I exaggerated. "You will grow up and have babies."

She thought for a moment. "I am not that far," she said with relief. "Will you die?"

"No, not for a very long time." I didn't exaggerate.

I wished that there were better ways I could help my children master their fear of death, but I knew that honestly answering their questions to temper their vivid imaginations and reassuring them of our longevity was the best that I could do. I was glad that Marc and Lara were able to express their fears of death verbally. Sharing a fear with someone makes it less scary and facilitates our mastery over it. My children might have suffered more from their fears if they had hidden them from me.

I knew that mastering their fear of death did not mean that Marc and Lara would no longer have any fears about death. Mastery only means that we do not let our fears interfere with our living. Even as adults we have fears about death, but the healthy have learned to live with them. Time can attenuate fears, but not erase them.

As Marc and Lara became accustomed to asking questions and receiving my direct answers, it gradually became easier for them to admit their fears and to face the discomfort we all feel when we think about our vulnerability. At dinner one evening we were all munching on crisp strips of bacon when Lara contemplated what she was eating.

"Poor piggy," she lamented as she crunched. "Do they let some of the mommies and daddies stay alive to take care of the babies?"

"Yes, I'm sure they do," I guessed.

Marc wasn't satisfied with only a middle-age life span for the swine. "Well, do they let some of them die of old age?" he asked.

"Probably." What did I know about the sentimentality of pig farmers?

"Don't worry, Lara," Marc comforted. "It doesn't hurt to die. At least I don't think it does. You can't really wake up and say, 'Hey, it hurts to die!'" He thought for a minute about what he had just said. Looking me directly in the eye he softly admitted, "I'm afraid to die."

"Almost everyone is afraid to die when they are young, Marc," I pointed out. "But you don't really have to worry about dying yet. You have a long time yet. Most people live to be very old. Most people don't die when they are young."

Lara had been listening attentively. "Like Daddy?" she chimed in.

"Like Daddy."

Despite the relative stability of their environment after Don's death, both Marc and Lara expressed a concern about what would happen to them if I died. They no longer lived in blissful ignorance of mortality. If Daddy died, Mommy could die, too. And not only Mommy.

Lara reasoned one day, "If you die and Grandma dies and Granddad dies, I won't have any grown-up."

"There are lots of grown-ups who love you, like Aunt Barbara," I reassured her. "I won't die for a very long time. I'll be here to take care of you."

Even though I believe in my longevity, and I want my children to believe, too, we have discussed who their guardians are in the event that something unforeseeable should happen to me. They know, too, that a document—my will—exists to make sure that everyone else knows that they would go to live with their guardians. Because one of the main concerns of children after the death of a parent is whether their own needs will continue to be met, knowing that they will be taken care of even if the very worst should happen to them helps ease children's fears about the death of their surviving parent. Knowing that my will exists and clearly states my wishes makes me rest more easily, too.

Though Marc and Lara were progressing through the levels of cognitive development and refining their concept of death, they still had a long way to go before they could understand on an adult level. Both children would continue to ask a myriad of questions during our journey through the mourning process. Some of their questions would be emotionally wrenching for me to hear and answer, yet I answered them all as honestly as I could.

I must confess that my own concept of death, especially its spiritual dimension, also continues to expand. At the time of Don's death, my spiritual conviction had been badly shaken by our suffering and by witnessing the suffering of so many others. Except for my one comment about Don's spirit on the night of his death, I did not try to teach my children an adult spiritual concept of death. That comment had been intended more to alleviate Marc's fears of ghosts than to provide any spiritual solace to him.

Understanding death in the abstract is part of a fully mature concept of death and most adults who believe in a spiritual aspect of death hold those beliefs, at least in part, on an abstract level. When children begin to develop a spiritual concept of death, their questions and beliefs are formulated according to their level of cognitive development.

Marc was in the stage where his curiosity about the physical aspects of death carried over into a curiosity about spirituality, but on his own concrete level of thinking. Marc, like most children of his age, tended to wonder about the physical questions of spirituality. What is the spirit and the spirit world like and how does it compare with or interact with our world? It would take time for my children to work on the concrete aspects of death, before they began to feel the need for a well-defined spiritual belief. That future time, in fact, coincided with my own awakening spiritual needs.

In the beginning, Marc's spiritual concept was quite rudimentary and self-directed. Immediately after Don's funeral, as I climbed unsteadily back into my car outside the cemetery gates, my friend Melissa took one look at my grief-stricken face, and said, "Marc told me that you said Don's spirit would always be with him. I think that is a beautiful thought."

It *was* a beautiful thought. But one not easily accepted by a six-year-old boy. As the car rolled away from the cemetery, Marc asked me, "What is a spirit? Can you see it? Can you touch it?"

Too drained to go into long explanations, I answered too briefly, "No."

"Then I don't believe in spirits," my little scientist concluded.

A mere two weeks later Marc had reconsidered. His conversion to a belief in Don's spirit came from a source more convincing and definitely more imaginative than the words of his mother—the Star Wars saga. Marc had been especially engrossed in the original movie during the duel to the death between Obi-wan Kenobi and the evil, victorious Darth Vader. A miniature Star Wars buff, he had amassed a collection of tiny plastic figures and vehicles that was easily worth more than my jewelry. He played with them from morning until night, when I delivered his final drink of water to his bedside in a Star Wars paper cup. When the cup was empty, I always read him the little biography of the character pictured on the cup. This particular night that character was Obi-wan Kenobi.

When I finished reading about Obi-wan's "transformation" after his battle with Darth Vader, Marc asked, "What is *transformed*?"

"Changed," I answered with assurance. "He changed into a spirit. His spirit isn't in his body anymore, just like Daddy."

I chose to talk to Marc about my more adult, spiritual concept of death because I thought it would help him further differentiate himself from his deceased father, an important process for healthy mourning. The dead are different from us now because they have changed into something new. They are no longer a part of our world in the same way that they used to be.

I was hesitant to explain my belief that Don's spirit had separated from his body, because I knew that it would be a difficult concept for Marc to understand, since the idea that a parent's body can be in the grave at the same time that his or her spirit lives elsewhere is an abstract one. A friend suggested the simple yet wise explanation that, when a parent's body gets too sick or hurt to go on living on earth, the part of Daddy or Mommy that we all loved goes to be with God. But I was so angry with God for not saving Don's life that I was not willing to relinquish Don's spirit to him. I kept it with us where we needed it to be and Marc was surprisingly easy to convince.

"But Luke can hear Obi-wan's spirit," Marc protested.

"Can't you sometimes hear Daddy's spirit talking to you?" I asked.

"Yes," Marc pondered. "Luke only hears him in his mind."

"That's right," I encouraged. "Nobody else can hear him."

"But Luke can see his spirit," Marc said, comparing again.

I was grateful to George Lucas for providing the transparent apparition of Obi-wan in *The Empire Strikes Back*. "You can see Daddy's spirit in your mind, too," I suggested.

Still wondering about the continual presence of a spirit, Marc said, "But Daddy didn't like to go to school. He was too old."

I smiled. "Daddy always liked school. His spirit would go anywhere with you."

"Where is his spirit? All around the school room?"

Unsure, but deciding not to spread a spirit too thin, I answered, "No, just around you."

"Who is his spirit with?" Marc asked.

"Everyone Daddy loved," I answered simply.

"Did he love those people you cried with at Nana and Grandpa's house?"

"Danny and Melissa? Yes, but not the way he loved you and his family."

"Daddy can't help us now," he sighed.

"Yes, he can," I reminded him. "His spirit will always be around you to help you."

"How can he help us?" Marc questioned.

"Just by being there and loving us."

Marc, proud of his common bond with Luke Skywalker, never questioned the existence of Don's spirit again. Whether that belief in his father's spiritual presence and love would help Marc through the mourning process, I could only guess. But we needed all the strength that we could give one another as we tried to pull our lives together after Don died and for the following months and even years.

THE PHASES OF GRIEF:
SHOCK AND DENIAL, ANGER, AND BARGAINING

In her ground-breaking book, *On Death and Dying,* Dr. Elisabeth Kübler-Ross discusses her experience with terminally ill hospital patients. She concludes that terminally ill patients go through five stages in their reactions to impending death: shock and denial, anger, bargaining, depression, and acceptance. Since that book was published, many professionals have agreed that these stages are also useful in describing the mourning process of any human being who has suffered a loss, including the death of a loved one. These stages of dying—or phases of mourning— seem to be coping mechanisms that provide a way for us to deal with our losses. The phases are not as distinct from one another as the word *stage* implies, nor do they necessarily follow one another neatly in a sequential order. They can exist simultaneously and even disappear and reoccur at later periods during the grieving process, and unlike stages, which occur at generally predictable times, these phases last for different periods of time for each person.

The first phase, shock and denial, begins with an initial, temporary feeling of numbness. Very quickly the numbness begins to wear off, and the overwhelming thought is "This can't be happening to me." Because we believe so strongly in the immortality of ourselves and our loved ones, death takes on an unreal quality. Although denying the death of our loved one is actually the refusal to accept reality, it does serve a healthy purpose. Denial can act as a buffer against pain too great to withstand. Denial helps us buy time, time to go on with the necessities of daily life, and most important, time to prepare ourselves mentally to cope with our loss in other, more realistic, ways. For a short period of time, denial can help preserve our sanity.

When our constant confrontation with reality forces us to give up the denial phase, the second phase, anger, usually follows. This anger may be expressed not only as rage, but also as envy or resentment. The object of the anger may not necessarily have any direct connection to the loss if the anger is diffused in several directions. Widowed people experiencing this phase of grief are often angry with their dead spouses for leaving them in an awful predicament, angry with themselves and feeling guilty for allowing their spouses to die, angry with doctors for not being gods, and angry with God for not being a doctor. At the very least, most adults feel angry with fate, something we have been taught to believe that we can control. What have we done to deserve this pain? Life just isn't fair. Why are we suffering when other people, no better than we are and maybe worse, are leading perfectly happy lives? Why me? Why couldn't it have happened to them instead of to us? Anger is a typical response to the unexpected loss of control over our lives.

The third phase, bargaining, is making a deal. I made many promises to God when Don was fighting cancer. If God would only let Don live, I promised never to make scary, mad wishes to be single and care-free again. If God would let Don live, I would pray every day, instead of just when I needed a favor, and never spank my kids again. Don didn't live and I became single but not care-free, I prayed almost every day because I needed a favor, and I still spanked my kids once in a while when I couldn't take it any more.

My bargaining during Don's critical illness was for a cure, while the terminally ill, aware of the inevitability of their deaths, bargain for postponement. This phase necessarily manifests itself differently in the grieving process from the way it appears as a stage of dying.

As a phase of grief, bargaining usually takes the form of wishing for a reversal. After the death of a loved one such bargaining takes on a quality of fantasy: promises are made if only the terrible loss could be undone. Children, of course, are experts at fantasy, and the very young, who believe in the egocentric power of their wishes, have difficulty distinguishing it from reality. Older children and even adults know the difference between fantasy and reality, but may still cling in imagination or regression to the magical powers of fantasy. This may be particularly true if the bereaved person feels guilty and sees the death as a punishment for some "bad" behavior: if we promise to be good, we should no longer be punished.

Depression, that stabbing, painful longing and sadness, is the lowest period both adults and children go through in the grieving process. Yearning, pining, despair, emptiness—the list of words is endless. We may cry all the time or find ourselves needing to cry but unable to do so. We may search for ways to fill the terrible void left by the absence of our loved one and to relieve our pain. Some of these ways will be healthy. Some of them may not be. This phase seems to last forever. It erupts through the other phases when those coping mechanisms break down, leaving us only pure sadness.

The time may come when there seems to be only flatness, no hope, nothing to live for. A person who gave meaning to our lives has been lost to us, and we have yet to find meaning apart from that person. At this point friends and relatives often become frustrated and impatient, believing that the bereaved person should be back to normal. Something must be wrong or the griever wouldn't still be mired in depression. We may even begin to believe ourselves that something is wrong with us for still mourning our loved one, that we must be weak or crazy if everyone else thinks we should have recovered by now. Unfortunately, it is not widely known or accepted that the normal grieving process can take two to three years and sometimes longer.

Eventually, the flatness changes to hills and valleys as we begin to enter the final phase, acceptance. Acceptance involves detaching from our dead loved ones and a recognizing of all of those clichés everyone told us at the funeral that were absolutely no comfort then. Life goes on. Time heals. We begin to discover that life does have meaning in and of itself. The first time we successfully pull ourselves up the hill and out of the valley of despair, there is a tendency to think we have it made. We feel good and rejoice that the worst is over. Then something causes a setback and we slide down into another valley. The cause may be as slight as a bad day or as great as another loss. Sometimes we may not be able to pinpoint any one cause.

At first I reacted to these setbacks with shock, but eventually I gained confidence from knowing that I had dragged myself up that hillside before so I could do it again. In time, too, the valleys are not so low and are farther apart, with good times in between.

I am not sure that acceptance can ever be total. The death of a spouse or parent is an experience that most of us must live with for the rest of our lives. We learn to deal with our grief as it reappears later in life, but we never completely get over our loss. Yet there is a certain peace in knowing that we have survived. That is the normal grieving process.

Although it is easy to see the manifestation of these phases in most grieving adults, professionals and parents still wonder if children react to loss in the same way. Because children do not understand death on the same level that adults do, many people even ask if children mourn at all. The answer is emphatically *yes*—if they are allowed and encouraged to do so. When we shut children out of our grief in order to spare them our pain, we do them a great disservice. The message that it is shameful or weak to mourn delays children's mourning or leads them to repress their grief. Just as it is healthy for adults to work through the normal grieving process, mourning children need to express their feelings for the relief of their pain, too.

When children are inhibited from reacting to a loss, their grief may come out at other, less appropriate times, such as crying over the loss of a game. Their behavior may become antisocial and unmanageable or they may suffer continuous depression. Through the teenage years unresolved grief can contribute to the disruption of friendships, failing grades in school, promiscuity and pregnancy, and even drug abuse, delinquency or suicide attempts. A child's failure to mourn may have far-reaching consequences later in adult life, such as low self-esteem, and inappropriate aggression toward, or withdrawal from, others. Feelings of abandonment or rejection can also inhibit the ability to form bonds of intimacy, by keeping the unresolved griever at a safe distance from other people. Therefore, adults who have reacted to childhood bereavement stoically often have problems on the job, in their marriages, and with parenting.

As tempting as it is to try to protect our children from the painful feelings of grief, we cannot. It is impossible. Their grief will be expressed one way or the other, and it is far better to allow them to let it out so that we may guide and comfort them.

When children do express grief, their progress through the phases of mourning differs from that of adults. The onset of mourning in children may be delayed because their first concern is whether their needs will continue to be met adequately after their loss. Often their first reaction is to question whether their lives will otherwise continue normally. Once reassured, or at least once informed of impending changes, most children feel secure enough to begin mourning.

When children finally start to progress through the phases of grief, their emotions may be even less ordered than those of adults, showing many of the manifestations of grief rapidly and simultaneously. At other times they may take a break from grieving entirely, alternating brief but deep periods of sadness with a cheerful concentration on their normal activities. This has been called the "short-sadness span" by Martha Wolfenstein. As Joanne Bernstein explains in *Books to Help Children Cope with Separation and Loss*, "Youngsters find full immersion in grief overpowering. Fearing total loss of control, children are likely to grieve in short spurts, bouncing back to ebullience surprisingly soon."[1]

It is no wonder that children are uncomfortable losing control of their emotions during grief. From babyhood they are expected to master control over impulses ranging from elimination to temper tantrums. Denial, anger, and depression are likewise all "negative" emotions that parents have taught children to control in order to receive parental approval.

Adults, who more often experience the emotions of grief for extended periods, are sometimes intolerant of children's "inappropriate" happiness during mourning. Grown-ups must keep in mind that children are under tremendous stress when a parent dies. Adults have learned ways to cope with stress, ways that children have yet to learn. The short-sadness span is one way children reduce the stress of mourning, and in fact it may be the most appropriate way.

Other reactions children may have to the stress of mourning are aggression, temper tantrums, withdrawal, apathy, forgetfulness, hyperactivity, appetite changes, sleep disturbances, and regression. Mourning children may suddenly begin to have fistfights with friends, or they may stop playing with old companions altogether and spend most of their time alone. Some may take up a new set of friends whom parents and teachers may consider the wrong crowd. School grades may plummet because children don't remember their homework assignments or forget what the teacher explained in class, and what's more, they don't care. Some children will be in constant motion and therefore unable to concentrate. Others will seek refuge in food and gain weight or, just the opposite, will develop anorexia nervosa. Other grieving children may have nightmares or insomnia. If any of these symptoms becomes extreme enough to interfere with the psychological or physical well-being of the child, professional help should be considered.

---

[1] Joanne E. Bernstein, *Books to Help Children Cope with Separation and Loss* (New York: R. R. Bowker Co., 1983), p. 158.

Regression, a common reaction, is reverting to behavior displayed at an earlier age such as whining, bed-wetting, thumb or bottle sucking, clinging to a parent, or seeking the comfort of old toys or security blankets. It is often discouraging for surviving parents to watch their grieving children lose skills that they previously mastered. However, such regression should not be taken as a sign that the child is necessarily suffering permanent damage. It is normal and represents a usually temporary way that children cope with the stress of mourning. If parents allow their children to go back to a time when they felt more secure, young grievers will usually gain enough strength and comfort from that to progress again to their own age level. Their repeated practice at mastery may even make them better at their renewed skills. When parents try to pressure or ridicule children out of regression, however, they may only be increasing their youngsters' stress.

Marc and Lara, at various times during the aftermath of Don's death, clearly exhibited all of the phases and some of the stresses of grief in the typical manner of children. Although they seemed basically unaffected at the time of Don's funeral, six weeks later, they had exhibited most of the manifestations of grief in brief episodes. Their emotional reactions did not always come in a convenient order, so I could not say, "Aha! My children have now passed from stage-one shock and denial to stage-two anger." Denial could sometimes crop up in the midst of depression; even in acceptance, the sadness of depression lingered. There is no single, normal, orderly way for anyone, much less a child struggling to grasp the concept of death, to grieve. Marc and Lara both took their own paths through the phases of grief, leaping ahead at times, backtracking at others.

Don died on January 8, 1982. On January 10, we buried him. On January 11, we came home to an empty house.

The reality of Don's death was impossible to absorb completely, and while I struggled through my own shock and denial, I tried to be aware of the ways in which Marc's and Lara's behavior was a manifestation of the same struggle. I soon realized that shock and denial, anger, and bargaining, were taking turns and that each child also had moments of regression when these coping mechanisms proved insufficient to handle the tremendous pain and longing.

Sometime during our first night at home, Marc decided to make my bed seem less empty. I let him stay for a while, then tucked him back into his familiar bed. Early the next morning he shuffled into my room. "I want to go see . . ." He hesitated. "Granddad," he finished sadly.

"You really want to see Daddy, don't you?" I asked.

"Yes," he admitted, and trudged downstairs to find his grandfather for male companionship. I understood how hard it was simply to remember that Don was dead. My brain cells didn't want to store that information either. They short-circuited. Shock and denial were at least some protection from the pain.

Marc spent part of every night with me for days after Don died though he always went to sleep in his own bed. If I awoke before morning to find him sleeping next to me, I carried him back to his own bed. I hoped that by making that draining effort I would give him the comfort of my presence for a while without fostering any habits that would be difficult for him to break later on.

It wasn't Marc's weight that made that nightly trip between his room and mine one that I dreaded. It was that I was suffering the physical symptoms of shock. If I awoke in the night, which I frequently did, I was initially disoriented. I was deeply fatigued, partly because I wasn't sleeping enough, but also as a cumulative effect of bearing the stress of Don's illness for two years. I wasn't eating well, either, and lost over twenty pounds in the weeks before Don died and just after his death.

However, the most difficult physical problem for me was that I couldn't seem to keep warm enough. Even though I slept under heavy blankets and a comforter, I needed to wear a robe over my nightgown and sometimes two pair of socks to bed. I hated climbing out of bed to take Marc back to his room, because I knew that I would become quickly chilled and that it would take me minutes if not hours to warm up enough to sleep again. I forced myself to take him back to bed every night anyway.

Exactly one week after Don's death my emotional insulation began to crack. As if ruled by some internal time clock, my body started to tense up about four p.m., anticipating the hour Don had been struck by the fatal hemorrhage. From then until about seven, my eyes searched out the clock every five minutes as if I were waiting for an execution. I wasn't even sure of the exact time of Don's death, but when darkness fell, the waiting was suddenly over and I relaxed somewhat. That night Marc's visit began and ended early, so I was alone in bed until my son came in to snuggle with me the next morning.

"I came in because I thought you might be lonesome and miss Daddy," he said.

"You miss him, too, don't you?" I asked.

"Yes." I was glad that he could admit to sadness, a step toward progressing beyond denial.

After he left to get dressed, I heard Lara stirring in her bed and dragged myself into her room to pick her up. Holding her tightly, I ducked back into my bedroom to slide my feet into my slippers. Lara looked at the other side of my bed. The comforter was still neatly stretched across the fluffy pillow. Obviously, no one had slept on that side last night. Lara was shocked.

"Daddy isn't here!" she exclaimed with surprise. "He's dead."

Eight mornings had passed and we still did not want to remember. Marc had happily returned to school and his normal activities as though nothing had happened. Yet each night he was running to his parents' bed, a regressive behavior that brought him comfort from his unexpressed fears. Lara, too, seemed happy most of the time, except when she occasionally cried and complained that she missed her father. Then, she sought comfort from the toys of her infancy. All I felt was a tremendous void, as if outer space had moved inside of me; Don's mortality was inconceivable to me. When I had to say to Lara, "He's dead. He can never come back," I got the same feeling I used to get when I said to Don, "You won't die." Deep down inside there was a little part of me that didn't really believe it, and I had to push away the uneasiness that accompanied my self-deception.

Lara and I snuggled for a while until Marc popped in

again, complaining of hunger. We had breakfast while my mother still slept. My father, the early riser, had gone home so my mother had no one to rouse her if I kept the children quiet. As Lara sat in her high chair slowly finishing her breakfast, I shuffled around the kitchen putting food-smeared plates directly into the dishwasher. I didn't have the energy to scrape them. Marc crawled underfoot, racing his miniature cars across the smooth kitchen floor. The metallic click of their wheels grated on my nerves, but I didn't say anything. One of Marc's cars skittered off course and crashed behind the trash can. He pushed the light plastic can aside to retrieve his toy.

"There's red there!" He pointed to low spots under the cupboards and on the side of the stark white refrigerator. "It must be Daddy's blood." He drove his cars to the other side of the room while I knelt on all fours to check out Marc's discovery. The spots were indeed Don's blood, which the rescue squad had missed cleaning up, since they hadn't stooped to a child's eye-level. I wet the kitchen sponge to wipe up the rest of my husband's blood and wash it down the sink. I shivered, trying to shake off this intrusion of reality into my protective state of shock. None of us said another word about it. We went on with our day as if the incident had merely been a bad dream.

"A dream is a wish your heart makes, when you're fast asleep," sings Walt Disney's Cinderella. Psychologists tell us that dreams are also expressions of our unconscious thoughts. Marc had not yet wept aloud in his grief, but he began to have dreams about his father, perhaps because it was safer to face his loss in the unreal world of dreams than to admit his feelings of grief directly to me.

One evening Marc's final words to me before drifting off to sleep were, "I miss Daddy." When he bounced into my room to wake me up the next morning, he glanced at the empty half of my bed and ignored the space. "I had a dream about Daddy," he cheerfully announced. "I was checking on everyone and Daddy was sleeping. I know he was sleeping because he was snoring."

A few days later Marc had a similar dream, but this time he acknowledged the concrete evidence. In the morning when he crawled into bed with me to snuggle, he said, "When I got up for a drink of water, I had a dream about Daddy. I dreamed that he was sleeping with you. I was sad when he wasn't."

I surmised that Marc's dream may actually have been a daydream. I wondered if he had other daydreams about his father, as I did. "Do you ever dream that he is awake and playing with you or reading to you?"

"Yes." Did he answer "yes" only to please me? "I miss Daddy," he sighed.

"I miss him, too. Do you ever cry when you miss Daddy?" I was concerned that I hadn't yet seen Marc's tears.

"No," Marc paused to reconsider. "Yes, tears in my eyes," he explained.

Tears in his eyes I understood. That's exactly how I felt, because the hurt was too shocking, too deep for any other kind of tears.

"I do, too," I said to let him know we shared similar feelings, but it evoked no further revelation from him. He pulled himself together to get on with his day.

"Let's get up," he advised. We did.

About a month after Don's death, I began to worry about Marc because his denial seemed to be increasing rather than diminishing. He still hadn't cried and at times he refused to talk about Don's death or listen to anyone else talk about it either. I knew that he must be bottling up a lot of his emotions, one character trait we shared. I, however, had the advantage of being more verbal, so that I could express my feelings in words, if not in tears. Marc's way of expressing himself was predominantly through action.

Don's basement study had been left pretty much intact. I had added a few things to his desk after I picked up his personal effects from his office. Marc had often visited his father at work, so I wasn't surprised when he brought a many-sided plastic calendar-ball and a fuzzy troll knickknack from Don's office up to the living room to play with. If playing with Don's possessions gave Marc comfort, I was glad that he had felt free to touch them.

Lara also looked approvingly at her older brother and stated, "Daddy doesn't need them anymore because he's dead."

Marc turned on her and hissed, "Don't say that word 'dead'!"

I didn't know what to do to help Marc face the facts. I only worried more.

Two days later at the breakfast table I was scared into saying at least a few words.

As usual Lara started the day with, "I miss Daddy."

"Don't say that word," Marc barked. Lara hadn't said "dead."

"What word?" I asked.

"Daddy," Marc said with a wince.

I could no longer ignore Marc's denial. "Marc, we have to talk about Daddy," I insisted. "Someday we will be happy when we talk about Daddy." I felt compelled to say the objectionable word over and over again, trying to condition the pain out of it for my son. "We will remember the good times we had with DADDY!" Though my voice rose in volume to almost a scream, I still wasn't sure that Marc had heard, since he had covered his ears, pressing the palms of his hands against them with enough force to block out the painful sound. I couldn't persist, but both my son and I were already too agitated to finish breakfast. Marc went to the living room to watch "Sesame Street" while I cleaned up Lara.

Until the time came when Marc could finally cry for relief from the denial, about all I could do was keep communication going and continue to reinforce reality as gently but firmly as I could. Sometimes I had to remind myself that my task wasn't to push Marc through the denial phase faster, but to support him in whatever phase he was in. As much as I wanted to, I could not "cure" my child. I could, however, care for him so that the security of my love could help him heal from within his own soul with time.

I tried to be patient and to take comfort in knowing that my children still acted as happy as normal most of the time. They even looked forward to things that would bring them pleasure, something I was unable to do. In fact, I was dreading a trip to Disney World that Don and I had planned for February and I'd hastily rescheduled for the week after school got out. Marc and Lara had taken the postponement with little fuss because their grandparents would now be able to meet us there. Both children seemed oblivious to my negative attitude as they talked about summer vacation with excitement.

One day Lara asked me, "When we go to Disney World, can I go on the cups-and-saucers ride?"

I tried to answer cheerfully, "Sure, we can all go on them: Mommy, Marc, Lara, Grandma, and Granddad."

"But Daddy can't go." Lara noticed the omission in my list.

"No, but he went on the cups-and-saucers when we went to Disneyland." I wanted her to remember that Don hadn't missed out on her fun completely.

"I miss Daddy," she sighed in a by now familiar refrain. "I want to give him a hug and a kiss."

"So do I, but we can't," I gently reminded her.

"Why?" Lara asked seriously.

Wishing she could understand, wishing she didn't need to deny the truth, wishing I didn't have to say it yet again, I said it. "Because he's dead."

"Why is he dead?" she persisted. "I don't want him to be dead."

"I don't want him to be dead and he didn't want to be dead either. He got very sick and the doctors couldn't fix him."

"He should take some medicine," she prescribed. She had just swallowed half a teaspoonful of sticky strawberry decongestant herself.

"He can't take medicine after he is dead. Medicine wouldn't have helped him anyway. He was too sick. He didn't have just a cold, like you."

Like Don's cancer, Lara's cold and her mourning would have to run their course. Probably her denial was as much a result of her limited understanding of death as it was a defense mechanism. Because she didn't understand that death is irreversible, she would have to struggle for a few years, waiting for Don to come to life. Eventually she would accept that he wasn't coming back.

Cruel reality began to chip away at my own denial, at times refusing to let me ignore the truth. Valentine's Day was fun for the children because they came home from school with

lots of heart-shaped cards and candy. For me it was agony. I
sent a few cards to elderly relatives, but I had to catch myself
when I signed them. My hand automatically wanted to write,
"Love, Linda, Don, Marc, and Lara." My mother bought me
some red argyle knee socks and a box of candy from the
children, but there was no romantic dinner for two. Well, there
hadn't been last year either. Don had just gotten out of the
hospital after surgery. He hadn't been able to shop for a gift
then, but a lithograph that he had ordered for me and promptly
forgotten about just happened to be delivered the day before
Valentine's Day, much to his relief. This year, on the same day, a
copy of *TV Guide* addressed to Mrs. Donald Alderman arrived
in the mail. Marc, proud that he had kept the secret, confessed
that Daddy had ordered it for me as a surprise. It was a
shocking surprise!

A few days after Valentine's Day I ran into my neighbor,
Penny. We had spent a lot of time together each summer while
our children played after dinner, but we saw less of each other
in winter. This winter we were both occupied separately with
our grief. A few weeks before Don died, Penny's in-laws had
been killed in a head-on collision with a drunk driver. She told
me that just last night she had been relaxing in the bathtub
when she suddenly began to cry uncontrollably. She just
couldn't stop until the water finally got cold. Reality hits you at
those times when you least expect it, times when you are doing
automatic things. I'd been struck by it while waiting for Marc's
bus, while driving, while folding laundry. Often I grabbed four
forks to set the table and suddenly realized that the fourth one
was for my mother and not for Don.

The differences between present and past realities continually confronted me in trivial guises, making any attempt at
denial intermittent at best. As I made our bed, I flashed back to
going to the movies with Don. John Travolta had the same
Sears catalogue bedsheets in his trailer in *Urban Cowboy*. Now
I had no one to take me to the movies. It was something so
simple, something I had taken for granted. When I opened
Lara's curtains in the morning I thought of the day Don and I
picked out the fabric from among the many remnants at a mill

in Pennsylvania. Now I had to shop alone. It became impossible for me to maintain denial for long. My loss was just too real.

But for a long time there were still instances when I would momentarily slip into the past. One Saturday morning as I cooked our ritual breakfast of pancakes I thought I heard Don's slipper-muffled footsteps coming down the stairs to join us. I expected to see Don, clad in his bathrobe and pajamas, sit down at his chair and wait for his pancakes. The bowl of mix was empty, and for a moment I felt as if I should be cooking more.

Eventually I was able to laugh at the little tricks my mind played on me. I was seldom able to laugh, though, when I witnessed my children suffer after I thought they had moved on to expressing their grief in other ways. A long time into our mourning I overheard Lara revert to a disturbing, yet classic, instance of denial. She was playing downstairs in our playroom with Penny's younger son, Grant. I was dressing in my room to go out when I heard Lara's footsteps rapidly thumping up the stairs. She headed directly for the bathroom, so I thought she had waited until the last minute to go again. Then the door quickly slammed and the footsteps raced back down the steps. What was she up to, I wondered. Then I heard her yell, taunting, to Grant in the playroom, "My Daddy's upstairs in the bathroom getting dressed, so you can't see him!"

Watching my children suffer through the second phase of grief, anger, gnawed at me every bit as much as their denial had troubled me. Although I knew that my children would at times be angry about their father's death, I railed against their fits of temper. Anger was an emotion that I had tried to teach them to control so that they could make friends and be well-liked. I had usually punished their outbursts, at least by ignoring them and sometimes by sitting them down alone for a tongue-lashing and a time out. To some degree, then, Marc and Lara must have been at war with themselves whenever they felt anger welling up in them as a reaction to their father's death. It is scary enough to lose a parent, but even scarier to then feel something that, if expressed, could bring angry words from the only parent they had left. I tried to be more tolerant of my children's anger after Don died, realizing that it was a natural phase of the grieving process.

Lara was not, by nature, an angry child. She generally accepted calmly whatever came her way. A broken toy might elicit tears, but not an urge to punch the offender. I heard her get really angry with grief only once. She was about to lie down for her nap one day when her approaching sleep made her think of her supine father. "Daddy's resting in his case," she commented. She glanced at my face as I bent closer to tuck her in. "I can see your nose get bigger."

"I'm breathing," I explained. "You are, too, but it's hard to see your own nose."

"I can see your nose and Marc's nose, but I can't see Daddy's nose. He won't ever come back."

"No, he won't."

"Maybe someday he'll come back."

"No," I disagreed firmly. "He won't ever come back."

"I miss my daddy," she cried.

"I miss him, too."

Then my gentle little girl curled her small hands into tight fists and beat them against her mattress, wailing loudly in anguish, "I want my daddy! I want my daddy!"

I wrapped my arms around her tightly and rocked her until she finally dozed off to sleep.

Marc was more prone to express his anger, both verbally and physically. But unlike some bereaved children, he did not become physically abusive or uncontrollably disobedient. Perhaps because we talked so openly about the troubling details of Don's death and death in general, Marc's anger was attenuated.

That does not mean that he did not at times feel deeply angry. In fact, Marc's anger erupted in many directions, as is common with bereaved children. Some are furious with their dead parent for deserting them, and it is important for the surviving parent to tell the children that their parent didn't want to die and leave them. Children still may have thoughts like, "If he loved me, he'd have been more careful and not gotten into an accident," or, "If she loved me, she'd have taken better care of herself when she got sick." Again, reassurance is called for from the surviving parent.

Even suicide can be explained in a way that assures children that their parent did not die because of a desire to leave them personally. There may still be no way to forestall anger at the dead parent, however, because the child must be told that the parent made a poor choice trying to escape pain, either physical or mental, in a way that causes pain to so many other people. The suicidal parent wasn't thinking of that. The best way to end pain is to ask for help from someone who can help heal the pain, like a doctor can help heal the pain in our bodies.

Children may also resent their surviving parent for allowing the other parent to die or for not being able to fill the role that was left vacant by the death. Some children are angry at themselves, expressed usually as guilt. Anger directed at siblings or friends may disrupt any remaining semblance of normal daily life. Just as adults may be angry with fate, children, too, can be angry at the circumstances of their lives, especially when comparing life now with how it used to be. Unexpressed, such a feeling of being cheated may fester, causing problems later.

In the beginning Marc fumed if anyone violated his father's territory. At breakfast one morning he looked at his plain piece of toast and asked for butter instead of the orange marmalade that everyone else was eating. "That's Daddy's jelly," he objected.

"He wouldn't have minded if we used it," I reminded him.

"Yes, he would!" he insisted.

The next night at dinner Marc said to his grandmother, "You can't sit in Daddy's chair."

"Yes, she can," I said, embarrassed. "Daddy wouldn't have minded."

"Yes, he would." Marc was stubborn.

"He would have wanted me to be close to you," Grandma suggested as she sat down.

Marc scrutinized the seating arrangement around the

table. "I want to sit next to Lara," he insisted. "I'm tired of this seat." The seat next to Lara was the disputed one. If anyone was to sit in Don's chair, Marc wanted to be the one. I told Marc that he could sit in Daddy's chair after Grandma went home. Grudgingly, he accepted the compromise.

One day I was taken by surprise when Marc's anger was directed at me. The morning had started off as usual. Marc crawled into bed with me, this time wanting more than a cuddle. He needed comfort.

"I'm sad." He sniffed.

"Do you miss Daddy?"

"Yes." He sniffed again.

"I miss him, too."

Suddenly Marc leaped up and rushed downstairs to waken his grandmother. I heard only the first sentence he shouted, but it revealed what had driven him away from me so urgently.

"I wish Mommy were gone, not Daddy!" Marc's words burned in my ears. This was one of those awful mornings when my wish and Marc's were the same.

Later my mother told me what she had said to her grandson to cool his anger. She reassured him that his mother loved him very much and that she had loved his father equally as much. She reminded him that Mommy had taken Daddy to special doctors all the way in New York City to try to save his life. She pointed out that it wasn't Mommy's fault that Daddy died. Mommy just couldn't help it, and Daddy couldn't either. He didn't want to die and Mommy didn't want him to die. They had loved each other very much.

Then she talked to Marc about his parents' wedding, how happy everyone had been, especially Mommy and Daddy, how full of dreams for a joyful life and happy children they had been. Marc and Lara had only been a twinkle in Mommy and Daddy's eyes then. Yes, Mommy had loved Daddy very much and had not wanted him to die.

Marc listened to the recounting of the family legend and gradually calmed down. Then he came back upstairs to my bedroom and snuggled happily with me until it was time to get up.

That night Marc gave up his nocturnal visits to my bed and slept the whole night through in his own bed for the first time since his father died. Perhaps hearing from another person how much Don and I loved each other and how much we both loved him helped him to believe that his father's death was no one's fault. No one was to blame, and we could all sleep with a clear conscience, secure in the knowledge that we were loved.

I was relieved that Marc was making progress and that I no longer was burdened with carrying him back to bed each night. If I had expected regressive behavior from either of my children, it was Lara in whom I assumed it would have occurred. She was so young and had just mastered many of the skills of toddlers. Independent Marc had surprised me with his need for more closeness with his mother at night.

Just as Marc was reasserting his independence from me, it became clear to both my mother and me that her mission had been accomplished. She had helped with the children and the chores, and now it was time for me to stand on my own two feet. Shortly after Valentine's Day, we took her to the airport limousine and waved good-bye to her.

I felt quite confident until the weekend after she left. On Friday evening, after I tucked the children into bed, I momentarily panicked. Two long days with my children home from school loomed ahead of me. What will I do? I asked myself. The answer finally hit me and I calmed down. I would do all those things that I used to do, only I'd do them alone. I had no choice. I'd had five weeks of practice with my mother there. Now I would have to solo.

One consolation was that Marc seemed better able to handle his occasional moments of anger now. He never blamed me again for his father's death after my mother's talk with him, but I was concerned that he might turn his anger inward. I didn't want my son to feel guilty for his father's death in any irrational way.

Mr. Rogers sings a song to his young viewers to reassure them that their "crazy, mad wishes" are not responsible for any harm that later befalls the object of their wishes. Children can suffer tremendous guilt over a parent's death when, either silently or out loud, they have wished that parent dead in a moment of anger. What child hasn't been irate with a parent for denying a toy, for spanking the child, or for simply putting the child to bed against the child's wishes. Although adults know that children do not mean it when they say, "I wish you were dead," children sometimes have their doubts. Because children are egocentric, they also exaggerate their own powers of cause and effect. When a parent does die, they feel guilty.

I had never heard Marc wish that his father were dead, but I learned that he had another reason to feel guilty about his death. When Don had suddenly hemorrhaged in our kitchen, Marc and Lara had been watching television only feet away in our living room.

"I heard Daddy yell 'help,'" Marc finally confessed to me one day.

This news shocked me profoundly—perhaps because I had not been there myself and had only been told of Don's plaintive cry later. "There was nothing you or anybody else could have done, Marc," I assured him. "Nobody knew that Daddy's blood tube would break. We knew that he had something growing inside him that shouldn't be there, something called cancer, but we didn't know that it would make a hole in his tube." I repeated the cause of Don's death to drive home to Marc that, even had he responded to Don's cry, his father would have died.

"Why didn't you stay with us and let Grandpa go to the hospital with Daddy?" Marc challenged me.

"Because I am Daddy's closest relative, his next of kin. When someone is very sick, the doctors need to talk to the next of kin about what should be done to try to save the patient's life. I had to go. I was sorry to leave you and Lara, but you were with Nana and Grandpa," I explained.

Then Marc voiced a source of anger even greater to him. I had broken a promise. "Why didn't you bring us McDonald's hamburgers like you said you would?" It still grated him that I hadn't delivered the hamburgers the night his father died.

I almost laughed at my child's perspective, but I exercised restraint. "I was at the supermarket when Nana called me to tell me to come straight home because something was wrong with Daddy. It happened so fast that I didn't have time to stop at McDonald's. I'm sorry," I explained.

Little by little, at different times, Marc confided to me about his continued feelings of guilt and helplessness in not coming to the aid of his father.

"The book *When People Die* said that it doesn't hurt to die," Marc remembered one evening. "Why did Daddy say 'help' if he didn't feel anything?"

"Because he probably felt like he had to throw up. Then, when he started bleeding, he felt faint and wanted help." I tried to imagine, but not too vividly, how Don must have reacted to a massive pulmonary hemorrhage.

"I saw Daddy when he was a little bit alive and blood was coming from his mouth," Marc admitted sheepishly.

"I thought that you were in the other room watching TV." God, I wished I had been there to protect my children.

"I peeked," Marc softly confessed.

I hugged Marc to reassure him. "It's all right if you looked. Were you scared?" I knew that I would have been terrified.

"Yes," he answered honestly.

"Did you cry?"

"No."

"I cried at the hospital because I was scared." I made my own confession.

"I thought Nana was going to die, too," Marc said.

"People do different things when they're scared," I explained. "Nana fainted and I cried."

"I tried not to think about it," Marc stated coolly.

Marc would continue to be troubled by Don's death scene for a long time after his father died. I had often repeated to the children that Don didn't want to die, so that they would not feel angry at him for deserting them. I would never let them forget how much he loved them. Yet it hadn't occurred to me that Marc might get angry with Don for dying in a way that upset Marc and disturbed his routine.

"I wish Daddy hadn't made so much noise yelling 'help' and all the people coming to the house," he complained one day when he was tired and cranky. The entrance of the rescue squad must have been horrible for a six-year-old to witness and to remember. "I was trying to watch *Scooby-doo*. Grandpa shouldn't have told Nana that he was dead. She fainted."

"She fainted because she was sad," I reminded him.

"Well, I'm not," he boasted.

"Maybe not now, but you were."

The next day Marc sat down in front of the TV at his usual time to watch his favorite program. The cartoon had scarcely run beyond the opening title when he leaped up and switched off the set.

"This is the *Scooby-doo* I was watching when Daddy died. It was impossible to hear!" he stated with disgust. "I'm going to take Saskia for a walk." He fetched the dog leash and banged out the front door. My mouth fell open in amazement. When Marc misbehaved, the severest punishment that I could mete out was to take away even five minutes of his Scooby-doo time. Not only that, but my son had never in his life taken the dog out for a walk.

Sometimes Marc was angry with me for punishing him or denying him his wishes. Over time the memories of the deceased parent get glossy. I wanted my children to remember how good their father was to them, but sometimes I suffered in comparison. Once in a while when I said "no" to Marc, he got angry enough to shout, "I wish Daddy were here, not you." At those times, I agreed with him.

Eventually Marc's anger toward me surfaced more at times when I had difficulty filling in for his father. Initially he was quite patient with my fumbling attempts and even enjoyed his masculine superiority in certain skills. When I couldn't get my video game tank to avoid bumping into obstacles he would steer his tank and issue directions simultaneously. "Push your joystick up now, Mom." He would silently fetch his baseball when I pitched it five feet from his waiting bat. Marc enjoyed my companionship, and I had fun, too, taking his absent father's role in these non-threatening ways most of the time.

Sometimes, though, both Marc and I grew tired of the extra demands Don's absence placed upon us. I didn't know which of my children was cheated more: Marc, who had painfully clear memories of the good times he'd shared with his father, or Lara, who'd barely had any of Don's time at all. We all missed his companionship sorely.

As the season began to change, my own shock and denial crumbled completely and my episodes of anger grew as virulent as the children's. One day I screamed shrewishly at Marc from the stairs. I don't even remember what his transgression was, though it nudged me over the edge from control to hysteria. Marc retreated across the living room in fear, trying to escape me. "Daddy, Daddy!" he moaned softly. But when he reached Daddy's favorite chair, Daddy wasn't there. What was there was a worn Winnie the Pooh that had been Marc's security since babyhood. "Teddy!" he gasped as he clutched his bear for comfort. Then I turned my anger inward, feeling guilty for losing patience with my child.

Rancor made my sleep as fitful as shock had and I often lay awake waiting for morning. One restless night I wrote in my journal, "I've been bothered by thoughts of the grave. I hate spring this year. I look out in the backyard and feel that the grass and bushes have no right to grow again, to get green. They should be dead, too." Another line from the *Song of Songs* that had been read at our wedding kept popping into my head. "Arise, my love, my fair one, and come away. For behold, the winter is past." But Don could not arise.

Spring in New Jersey that year was unusual. Severe snowstorms kept interfering with the typical spring melt. One day when a heavy squall canceled school, Marc and I sat in the living room looking out the picture window at the falling snow. On a branch, looking at us, sat a lone, bright-red male cardinal. I had an overwhelming feeling that he was Don watching over us. The cardinal was absolutely still, as if waiting for us to move away from the window first.

Marc asked, "Is he d-dead?" He still had trouble saying the word.

It was so odd, that bird sitting there in the driving snow. I'll keep feeding the birds, for Don, I vowed.

Although comforting, the presence of the bird was hardly enough to make up for the resentment I felt over my loss. On one of the snowy days of spring I climbed into a hot, steaming bathtub to relax and get warm. I had barely lowered my tired back into the water when the vision of Don soaking in the tub after radiation therapy to prevent skinburn flashed into my brain. My back muscles tensed and I climbed out of the water, angry that even the refuge of my bathtub had been invaded by my loss.

In the craziness of widowhood that Lynn Caine describes in her book, I was unable to empty the scraps of paper in Don's wastebasket until April because they bore his handwriting. That accomplishment gave me the courage to wash our bedsheets for the first time on the following day. As I stripped Don's side of the bed, I found that the bottom sheet was covered with the short, black hairs he had shed during his chemotherapy. I got a plastic sandwich bag from the kitchen and began plucking them off the bed and dropping each one into the bag. I had barely begun this tedious process when Marc walked in on me unannounced. He looked at me quizzically and said, "What are you doing, Mommy?"

What was I doing indeed? Enraged that Marc had caught me in the act of craziness, I screamed at him, "Get out of here and leave me alone. Get out!"

He backed out of the doorway, his eyes open wide, and closed the door on his deranged mother.

I returned to methodically picking up each hair until my fingers ached. Swearing, I stripped the sheets and stuffed them into the laundry basket. So much for spring cleaning.

As surely as spring would come, whether I liked it or not, nature asserted herself in us with growth. While we continued our progress through the phases of denial and anger, there were times when our common loss brought us together in deeper ways than we had known before.

For Passover I planned to take the kids to Connecticut to visit Don's parents. I also wanted to pick out the monument for Don's grave. Unfortunately, it started snowing the day before we were to leave and continued for several days. The April storm took everyone by surprise and made the drive to Connecticut too hazardous. Marc's Easter vacation from school wound up lasting two weeks instead of one.

Toward the end of spring vacation I decided to take a day trip by train to Connecticut to pick out Don's tombstone myself. Don's parents took me to the cemetery for the first time since the funeral. There was a little plaque with his name on it, but no middle initial. The grave looked too short. I just couldn't believe he was under there.

I recoiled at the barrenness of the grave and realized that the children would probably feel the same way. There should be flowers and a tombstone on a grave. What would Marc and Lara want their father's grave to look like? I wondered.

When I returned home, I sought Marc's advice on the wording of Don's monument. He was immensely pleased and helpful. We decided that the greatest accomplishment in Don's life, and the one he had been most proud of, was being a father to Marc and Lara. I asked Marc how he felt about having his name on the tombstone just in case he feared that it might portend his own death. The thought didn't bother him, and he was pleased to be immortalized with his father. Lara, not really understanding the question, agreed because Marc agreed. So we drafted a hand-printed version of Don's tombstone on a piece of Marc's notebook paper. Under the Hebrew letters that spelled Don's Jewish name and date of death we wrote:

DONALD LEWIS ALDERMAN
BELOVED SON AND BROTHER
DEVOTED HUSBAND AND
FATHER OF MARC AND LARA
SEPT. 25, 1946–JAN. 8, 1982
THIS IS MY BELOVED,
AND THIS IS MY FRIEND.

Again we used my favorite two lines from the *Song of Songs,* verses that our two close friends had read dramatically at our wedding. As we had begun our life together with those words, so would we end it.

A few weeks later a rubbing of the engraving stencil arrived in the mail. Marc and I unfolded the large transparent sheet of paper together and checked the spelling and phrasing. More than satisfied, we gave our stamp of approval.

*   *   *

One day toward the end of April we casually began to use Don's chair at the kitchen table. Marc sat in it first one day at breakfast. He wanted to watch television through the kitchen doorway, just as Don had surreptitiously peeked to see the morning news.

Lara sat in the chair for our evening meal, and this time Marc made no objection. His anger seemed to have dissipated to the point where he had more control over his resentment. Lara took advantage of the opportunity to make an announcement. "I'm a big girl now," she said proudly. She refused to use her high chair any longer.

We had known all along that when Lara outgrew her high chair, someone would have to sit in the only vacant spot. But I had felt that Marc should be the one to decide in his own time so he wouldn't feel that he had to take his father's place. Even as I was relieved that the timing worked out right for both children, I also regretted that Don's chair was no longer Don's chair for them. To me, it will always be Don's chair, I thought.

I didn't anticipate that such a minor change would strongly affect me, but when I went to bed, reality hit me. I shouldn't have had that beer before bedtime, I told myself. It broke down my defenses. I lay in bed listening to my brain scream in rage, "No! Oh, no, Don, no!"

"I promise to learn my nine times nine and never sleep late or gobble my bread if I can see Daddy walking, and talking, and waving his hand, and turning his head. I will do everything you say if Daddy can be alive today." So says the popular little boy from Lucille Clifton's children's books in *Everett Anderson's Goodbye*.

Everett is eloquently expressing the third phase of mourning, *bargaining*. Of all the phases, bargaining seems to be the most irrational one. However, it works very well as a step between denying and accepting a loss. Bargaining recognizes the loss but refuses to accept it as final. The feeling says that we need only look around us to see that this is not how life is supposed to be. We keep wishing for things to be different. We keep hoping for that "happily ever after" ending. Older children, adolescents, and even adults, all beyond the stage of magical thinking, often regress to bargaining, too.

Children who feel guilty because they believe they magically caused the death of a loved one tend especially to believe in the power of bargaining. They may believe that they are bad and are being punished by their loss. If they are good, their loss will be reversed. To control those angry feelings that "caused" their loss, some shut off all feeling, inhibiting the grieving process. Others become anxious and distrustful of their thoughts, which leads to an inability to make decisions and a general state of confusion. They feel responsible for their loved one's death and therefore are responsible also for correcting that action.

When the parent has died of a lingering illness, some children are resentful because their failing parent can no longer share the things with them that they used to enjoy in health. Like adults, children may wish for the end to come so they can get on with their own lives. When the end does come, they want to take back that wish.

"A conscious or unconscious contract may be made," writes Claudia Jewett in *Helping Children Cope with Separation and Loss,* "a 'bargain' where the child acknowledges her helplessness to attain part of the goal without the intervention of a more powerful other—parent or deity. The child may promise to 'always be good,' or to 'wait forever,' or some variation on these. This fits snugly into children's normal magical thinking, and it is reinforced by fairy and folk tales—in order to get what you want you must strive diligently long enough or wait patiently long enough, and then the powers that be grant your wish."[2]

To my knowledge Marc and Lara never made promises to keep if their father could come back to life. Whether they made them silently or to God, as in most bargaining, I will never know. They did make wishes, even though deep in their hearts, they knew that wishes don't come true.

We treated ourselves to occasional candlelight dinners

---

[2] Claudia L. Jewett, *Helping Children Cope with Separation and Loss* (Harvard, Mass.: Harvard Common Press, 1982), p. 37.

when we needed a lift after Don died. The flames seemed to calm the children, and they liked to blow the candles out after dinner. One evening just before my mother had left to go home, Marc had decided that maybe our kitchen candles had the same powers as birthday candles.

"Come on, Lara," he said. "Let's make a wish. Let's wish that Daddy didn't die."

"You know that wish can't come true, Marc." I tried to discourage him.

Marc was not deterred. "Then I'll wish for a baby brother."

I gasped in horror. "That can't come true either."

"Then I'll wish for twin brothers, just like me." Twin brothers had been Marc's way of evening the score. There were three females in his home—Lara, grandmother, and me. Two brothers plus Marc would make three males, neatly replacing Marc's father for masculine companionship.

Even though Marc didn't wish again over candles for his father back, he wasn't convinced that there wasn't some other magic that could negate Don's death. One spring day as the snow finally began to melt he stared out our living room picture window contemplating a familiar stone structure as if he had never really noticed it before.

"Why do they call it a wishing well?" he asked.

"Because you can throw a penny in and make a wish," I answered.

"Can we do it in our wishing well?" Marc hoped with growing excitement.

"No, it doesn't have any water in it." For some reason I was sure that water was a requirement for a true wishing well. "But I'll take you to one this summer that does," I promised.

"Can I wish that Daddy is alive?" Marc beamed.

"No, because that wish can't come true," I answered regretfully. What good is a wishing well if you can only wish for what can come true anyway?

"Then can I wish to own a toy store?" Marc asked skeptically.

"Yes." That was more possible than his father's magical return.

Marc did finally give up wishing that his father would come back. Perhaps enough time had passed without his father for him to believe in the reality of his loss more than the fantasy of his wishes. Lara did not give up wishing with Marc, probably because she was younger and could not yet understand that death was final. At bedtime one night Lara remembered that she was ending another day without her father.

"I miss Daddy," she said again.

"I miss him, too, Lara." I hugged her.

"I wish I had a fairy godmother! I'd ask her to make my Daddy alive again."

"Oh, Lara, even a fairy godmother can't bring Daddy back to life." My heart cried for her. "When a person dies, he can never be alive again."

She ignored my insistence on reality. "I'm going to dream tonight that Daddy and you give me a toy pony," she stated with confidence.

I couldn't persist. "That sounds like a good dream," I agreed. If a little fantasy could give her a peaceful night's sleep, well, what harm would it be?

The first thing next morning Lara ran into her brother's room bragging, "I had a good dream last night!"

In order for me to be able to have good dreams at night I struck my own bargain. I knew that Don would never come back, but I promised to be a supermom if only Don's children could grow up to be healthy and happy. To many surviving parents the legacy of their late spouse's immortality is their children. I believed that Don could come back in his children, and I wanted to share with Marc and Lara my belief that their father still lived through them. I thought that it might bring them some comfort, as it comforted me. I did not, however, put any pressure on them to live up to their dead father's expectations. Don had always let them know that they could do that best by just being themselves.

One evening Lara toddled into Marc's room for their joint bedtime story. Since Marc was still vacillating between two books, she wandered over to his dresser to look at the photograph of her brother and her parents.

"We still have pictures of Daddy," she remarked.

Now an adamant believer, Marc chimed in, "And his spirit is still with us."

"Yes, and part of Daddy is in you, too," I added. I really didn't expect my comment to generate any questions because Marc and Lara had always been told that all babies had to have a mother and a father to be born.

Marc may have been worried that part of Don's cancer could be in him. "What part?" he prodded.

I told him that Don's part entered Marc before Don got sick. "When a baby grows inside its mother, part of the Daddy gets together with part of the Mommy to start the baby growing." No sooner had the words left my mouth than I knew that I was in for it. I cringed waiting for the big question. Marc didn't disappoint me.

"How does part of the daddy get into the baby?" he asked skeptically.

As a nursery school teacher I had given countless parents advice on how to tell their children the facts of life. As a newly bereaved parent my first thought was, "Why couldn't Don have waited a little longer to die, so he could have had this father-to-son chat with Marc?" In an awkward attempt at filling the vacant role of father in our family, I fumblingly explained to Marc about sperm and eggs and making love. Finally I promised to get some books from the library so that we could discuss any questions that Marc had later. I was sure that I must have left out something.

Marc had one more immediate question. "What would happen if someone who isn't married had a baby?"

I tried to emphasize that it could be hard for the mother. "She would have to raise the baby alone." I sighed over the imagined burden of some other single mother.

With empathy beyond his years, Marc reminded me, "And you know how that feels, don't you, Mommy?"

Looking from one to the other of my children, I could see Don's genes at work in their physical resemblance to him, especially in Marc. People often commented that he was the image of his father. When he came up with remarks like that, I wondered if he didn't have more of his father in him than just a few chromosomes.

Many months later when Lara would be old enough to share Marc's interest in reproduction, I'd tell her that I was very glad Don had given me a part of her when she'd started to grow inside me. "He gave a part of me to you, and you gave a part of me to him," she would say, to explain the ultimate act of love.

Did Don live on genetically in his offspring? Or spiritually in our knowledge of his love for us? And possibly in other ways as well? Perhaps bargaining is not so illogical after all.

During the last of the snowstorms that spring I was standing at the kitchen window one afternoon, musing about the scene outside. I have always liked the snow, always associated it with a warm cozy feeling of being sheltered inside. But this spring the prolonged storms seemed somehow malicious. As I watched the flakes swirling in the wind, I realized that each new flurry had taken me further back to January, closer to sorrow. I hoped that snow wouldn't always remind me of my greatest loss, of isolation and aloneness and feeling cold inside.

I walked to the living room window, and there in the yard I saw the bright red cardinal again, the same one that had watched Marc and me watching him. Perched on a barren branch, he was guarding three other muted cardinals while they fed.

$\mathcal{T}$HE PHASES OF GRIEF:
DEPRESSION

$\mathcal{T}$he fourth phase of grief, depression, seems to last forever, and, indeed, to some extent it does. Even in acceptance, long after one has put together a new life, depression can be triggered by a season, a holiday, or any other time when the longing for a loved one seems overwhelming. More than overlapping the previous phases, it is the undercurrent from which they are trying to protect us. Slivers of sadness pierce those defense mechanisms of shock and denial, anger, and bargaining from the beginning of our bereavement. Over time, those defenses loosen, and the dominant feelings become sadness and longing.

Marc expressed the slow-motion feeling of depression soon after Don died.

"How many days has Daddy been dead?" he wondered.

"Fifteen." I didn't have to stop and think. I was counting the days myself.

"No, forty-eight," he contradicted with assurance.

"It seems like a very long time, doesn't it?" I agreed.

Tears are the classic expression of depression. Other grieving widows have told me, "I cried every day for a year." I'd cried at times from the day Don died. Lara had cried hysterically in the car at Don's funeral. Marc did not cry openly. A couple of weeks after Don died I began to worry that holding in his sadness might hurt Marc more deeply in the long run than letting go of his tears ever would.

One morning as Marc snuggled with me in bed I asked him, "Do you ever cry when I'm not with you, Marc?"

"No. *You* don't cry," he stated matter-of-factly.

"Yes, I have, lots of times," I said defensively.

"I didn't see you," he said. Then he asked a question beyond his years. "Didn't you want us to see you?"

I was shocked. I hadn't even realized that I was holding back my tears in front of the children to protect them from my pain. I had apparently sent Marc the message that the urge to cry should be controlled rather than expressed. Somehow I had to let him know that tears were necessary for healing to begin. I just wasn't sure that I was strong enough yet to show him by example. At least I could tell him about my tears.

"I guess you just didn't happen to be around when I cried." I tried to sound casual. Remembering those first two dreadfully empty mornings when I sobbed uncontrollably, not even knowing or caring who was my witness, I wondered if Marc had been near me then. "The first morning after Daddy died Grandma comforted me when I cried, and the next morning Granddad held me in his arms when I cried. I cry when it hurts a lot. Lots of times tears come to my eyes when I open the cards people send to say that they are sorry Daddy died. I cry when I remember Daddy, too. Remember when you saw me cry with Danny and Melissa?" I knew that Marc had seen my tears then.

"Why?" he asked. I could tell by the tone of his voice that he was really asking: Why did you cry with them and not with me?

He was right. He deserved to share my grief more than anyone else. "They were our friends," I answered feebly. Just be patient, I told myself. He will cry in his own time.

But by the time my mother was preparing to go home a few weeks later, Marc still hadn't cried. I tried to think of some way to help him bring the tears to the surface. I had put off playing the tape of Don's second memorial service because I was afraid of breaking down when I heard my own voice echo the final eulogy for my dead husband. Just like my son, I feared that if I fell apart, I would be unable to put the pieces back together again. Ironically, I would have felt freer to drop into depression if I had had no children counting on me to care for them. The very children who needed the example of their mother's grief were the ones who inspired my repression.

My mother had missed the service at Don's company to baby-sit the kids. I had promised to play the tape for her. Finally, forced by my mother's impending departure I dragged the recorder out to the living room and played the tape. Finally, too, Marc watched me cry.

"Are you still sad that Daddy died?" he asked a few minutes after the tape ended.

"Yes," I sniffed.

"I'm not. I'm back to normal," he bragged, not quite the reaction I had hoped for.

The next day Marc checked again to see if twenty-four more hours had enabled me to recover. "Are you still sad about Daddy?" he asked again.

"Yes. I'll be sad for a long time," I repeated.

"I'm not," Marc insisted.

I tried not to show my consternation, sensing that Marc was holding his feelings down deep inside because losing control would bring an unendurable sadness. His short-sadness span was helping him cope with his loss. I trusted that he would stop protecting himself when he felt strong enough to stand the pain. Then he would cry.

One morning shortly after my mother left to go home I awoke in my darkened bedroom to the sound of my son's voice through the wall in Lara's room. "Today is our first rainy day without Daddy," he announced as he helped his sister out of her bed. After I settled the two of them in front of the television for Saturday morning cartoons, I crawled back into bed to drift into semi-sleep. For the first time I had clear, sensual memories of Don: how he felt, how he looked.

The sensation of his presence brought a flood of relief. I had been worried because, in the first days and weeks, I had tried to conjure him up and failed. That morning the memories were so vivid—concrete yet mystical—that I lay in bed for an hour with him, not doing anything, just being there, unconscious of passing time. I actually felt good when I got up. That was the first day that I wasn't overwhelmed by emptiness in the morning. It was going to be a good day. How long had it been since I had thought that? Even if it wasn't the same during the days that were to follow, at least I'd had one day.

Strangely, Don seemed to be with us all that day. As I stacked hot pancakes onto Marc's breakfast plate, he spoke to the air. "Sit down, spirit," he invited. "Daddy's spirit is sitting in his chair," he merrily explained to me. Then he sat in the spirit's lap.

"You've been thinking about Daddy this morning, haven't you?" I smiled at being in tune with my son.

"I've been wondering," he said. "When you are married to someone and they die, can you marry someone else?"

"Yes," I answered and waited for the big question.

"Will you marry someone else?" he asked.

My morning had been so special that Marc's question troubled me not at all. "Maybe someday, if I find someone I love as much as I love Daddy. But I won't want to marry someone for a long time, because I still miss Daddy too much." I didn't feel sad, though. I was still glowing.

"Oh." Marc's face fell with disappointment. "What will I do on Father's Day if they make presents for fathers? I don't have one!" His voice was close to panic.

"You have two grandfathers," I reminded him. "You can give your gift to one of them or you can take it to leave at the cemetery."

"I'll have to give it to Grandpa or Granddad because I don't have a father," he regretfully agreed.

Perhaps by dashing his hopes of finding a quick replacement for his father, I had unwittingly forced him to confront his longing for Don. At bedtime that day Marc and I sat on his bed while I combed his freshly washed hair.

"Daddy," Marc said looking at me. "You are Daddy!"

"No, I'm your Mommy," I insisted, as calmly and warmly as I could.

"No, you're Daddy!" Marc insisted.

"No, I'm Mommy," I repeated gently.

Marc exploded with painful despair. "I want Daddy!" he yelled. "I must have Daddy!"

I enfolded Marc in my arms, stroking his wet hair. "I know how you feel, Marc. I feel that way, too, sometimes, but he can't come back."

"Maybe he'll come back," Marc whispered hopefully.

"No, he can't come back."

Marc perked up slightly. "Yes, he can," he reminded me.

I don't know how I knew what Marc was thinking, but I did. "His spirit can be with us."

Marc nodded, seeming calm and content. I left him there while I took his comb back to the bathroom. No sooner had I dropped it off than I heard Marc crying loudly. Wondering if he had somehow hurt himself, I raced back to his room.

Marc sat where I had left him, sobbing with real tears. "Daddy! Daddy!" he cried with a hurt deeper than I could kiss to make well. I tried anyway. We hugged and cried together for the first time since Don died.

"It's all right to cry when we are sad," I sniffed when our sobs had subsided. "I miss him so much, too, Marc. We can cry together any time we feel like it. Oh, sweetheart, I love you so much!" My tears flowed as much for my child's pain as for my own sadness.

Marc gently patted me on the back to console me. "It's all right, Mommy."

Overwhelmed with love for my little boy, who at that moment reminded me so much of his empathetic father, I reached down to dry his eyes. "I'll wipe your tears and my tears on the same tissue," I said, and we laughed together between sob-caught breaths. As the beginning of the day had been good, so had the end. Marc had cried.

Marc did not cry again often, but I knew that did not mean he didn't miss his father as time went by. He and Lara showed other signs of depression that are more subtle than crying: sadness, longing, a feeling that something is missing, and an attempt to fill the void left behind.

Longing often occurs during daily routines when grievers encounter memories of incidents that were pleasurable in the past. Some of Marc's most pleasurable moments had been with his father, so it was natural that he would feel sad each time he did the things he used to do with Don. Because of her age, Lara had fewer memories of times shared with her father, but there were still instances when she felt his absence.

One way Marc attempted to cope with his longing was to step into Don's shoes, but he soon discovered they didn't fit. Much to my dismay, Marc reached a point of wanting to replace his father and become the man of the house. As he brushed his teeth for school one spring morning, Marc looked at the empty counter on the left side of the sink, formerly cluttered with Don's toiletries.

"Can I have Daddy's aftershave lotion that he got for Christmas?" he asked. I nodded. "I'll use it tomorrow morning when I shave." Marc moved his comb, toothbrush, and toy razor from the side of the sink he shared with Lara and me to the other side, making Don's side less vacant.

At bedtime Marc pressed a small piece of paper in my hand, saying, "Here is an important note for you." The message was a wobbly *S*. "It's to remind me to shave in the morning," he explained.

The next morning Marc and I filled the sink with water for him to shave. We quickly spread a thin layer of shaving cream on his face and "shaved" the foam off with his toy razor.

"It took Daddy longer to shave," he said, scowling. "Where's Daddy's shaving lotion? What would happen if I put shaving cream on top of my head?" He scrutinized his face in the mirror. "Would my hair fall out?"

I wondered if he thought that Don's hair had fallen out from the shaving cream rather than as a side effect of chemotherapy, but I didn't have a chance to ask. Lara popped into the bathroom dismayed that she had missed the fun. Once or twice Don had let Lara borrow Marc's toy razor, even though Marc had clearly resented her intrusion.

"When Daddy . . . when Granddad . . . next time I'm going to shave alone with no Daddy," she vowed. Like Marc, she didn't want to practice alone the ritual she'd shared with her father. Knowing her intrusion wouldn't be welcomed by Marc she turned to me and asked, "Will you stay with me?"

"Yes," I promised.

Marc didn't seem to like the idea that I would let Lara shave any more than he'd liked his father's attention to her during the male ritual. All morning Marc acted out his version of man of the house, becoming unusually bossy with Lara. She, in turn, grew more stubborn by the minute.

Finally, as he dragged her screaming and kicking into the kitchen for lunch, I lost my patience. "Marc, don't try to make Lara come to the table," I scolded. "You are not her mommy or her daddy. I am her mommy. I'll tell her what to do."

"Yes, I *am* her daddy," Marc proclaimed. "Now that Daddy died, I'm the daddy."

"No, you're not," I stated firmly. "Lara needs you to be her brother. No one can replace Daddy."

At bedtime Marc again offered, "I can fill in for Daddy."

"No one can replace Daddy," I repeated gently, hugging my little boy. "I need you to be my son."

"What good is a son?" His face saddened with dejection.

"You and Lara help me and make me happy when I'm sad." I stressed his importance. "I need to love you and for you to love me. We are a family."

In a family that is missing a father or a mother, the remaining relationships are lifelines. After that night Marc seemed more satisfied with his position in the family and he didn't try to play his father again. I was relieved by this and also thankful that no one else tried to influence Marc to become the man of the house, something doomed to failure. His shortcomings would increase rather than diminish his longing for the man he could never replace.

The memories of Don that brought sadness and longing for Lara were different from Marc's. In very young children memories are often triggered by the repetition of physical activities. For months after Don died Lara responded to a simple hug with the teasing statement that Don always made when he hugged her and wouldn't let go. "You're my teddy bear," she mimicked.

One day when I walked into the living room from the front hall she requested impishly, "Do what Daddy does when he comes home from work."

"What does Daddy do?"

"Like this," she instructed, kneeling on one knee and stretching her arms out to hug the air.

I was both amazed and comforted that Lara still remembered her father long after her separation from him, even though she often reacted with words and tiny tears. At first memories were wrenching for all of us, each one pointing out how much we had lost. But during times of depression, I tried to make our memories comforting. Though we could no longer share moments of pleasure with Don, the void could be partly filled by remembering the times we had enjoyed in the past. Remember Daddy Time was the first of several small things—mostly thought up on the spur of the moment—that helped to ease our longing and draw us closer together.

Photographs also helped fill the void of Don's absence. Shortly after Don died, I went through all of our old family snapshots and, for each child, picked out pictures of Daddy holding each baby in the hospital, bouncing them on his knee, and reading to them as preschoolers. I searched out the negatives to have duplicate prints made and bound them into inexpensive mini-albums that held twenty photos each. When the albums were assembled Marc and Lara had their own visual mementos of their relationship with their father from their birth through the Christmas two weeks before Don died. Sometimes they carried their albums around with various tiny toys in their sand pails. Sometimes they wanted to "read" their albums with me so that I could weave a story for each picture. Sometimes they wanted to look at their albums alone.

We also had portraits of Don all over the house. Less than three months before he died, we'd sat for our first formal family photograph. The portrait of the four of us posing in somewhat old-fashioned, stiff stances crowned our dining room wall. We had other pictures taken of each child alone with both parents. Marc and Lara kept their own picture with Mommy and Daddy in their rooms. I had really wanted those pictures to be of each child alone with Don, but I'd been reluctant to ask Don to pose that way, lest he think that I believed he might very well die. The photographer had taken just one pose of Don and me together, which I kept on the dresser in my bedroom.

It was this last picture that especially attracted the children. Lara once gazed at the photo and asked me dreamily, "Do you remember when you married Daddy?" Sighing romantically she added, "You married him because you loved him. We still love him."

The children had another important record of their father, this one a tape. The Hanukkah before Don died, Marc and Lara's big present was a tape recorder. Bless Fisher-Price for including a demo tape suggesting ingenious ways kids could use their new machine, such as interviewing their parents. Don had been self-conscious about answering gumshoe Marc's dogged questions, but he had complied because he would do anything to please his children. So Don's voice was immortalized on tape. His account of our holiday activities was interspersed with a witty comment or two to break the drama. Long after he died, Marc and Lara often giggled over the taped banter of their adoring father.

Don's personal possessions, small and large, also gained a significance to the children when he was gone. The familiar items came to represent both the father they missed and their own past with him. When Marc wanted to divvy up Don's Christmas-stocking presents, he was not simply acting like the classic greedy relative; he was fighting for his memories.

"What can Lara have of Daddy's presents?" he asked after he picked out his choice first. "I have this"—he clutched a small wall thermometer in his hand—"and you have the thing for your car." He had chosen a suction cup compass for me.

"She can have this record and dance to the music," I suggested. Don had loved to watch her dance.

Marc seemed satisfied as he went to his room to stick his thermometer on the side of his dresser. I was glad that I hadn't just thrown everything into Don's closet, which had become a repository for his possessions. I didn't feel strong enough yet to clean that closet out, but I was glad that I hadn't let some well-meaning friend take over the job right after the funeral to spare me the ordeal. My early impulses might have led me to get rid of some of his more ordinary things—his pencil holder, his desk blotter, his nail clippers—which we made ours, thereby incorporating Don's memory comfortably into our everyday lives.

Some things we could not keep. Don's car had to be sold. I was relieved that the young man who bought it seemed to be both responsible and tickled pink to buy the gaudy orange Toyota. As I watched Don's car pull out of our driveway for the last time, I couldn't ignore the clenching in the pit of my stomach, especially when Marc stuck his head out the door and yelled to me over the fading noise of the engine, "Tell him to take good care of it!"

The gifts Don had given the children for special and not-so-special occasions represented a link to important times in their relationship with their father. Toys they had outgrown, such as Marc's wooden stacking clock brought back from a business trip years ago, became room decorations. Often I heard Marc and Lara caution a playmate or each other to be careful with a certain toy because "it's special to me. My daddy gave it to me."

Sometimes a toy elicited a memory that otherwise would have been lost. One day Lara asked me, "Do you know where my doggy is that Daddy bought me when he bought Marc's grasshopper? I want it!" We searched her "treasure drawer" until we found the small black-and-white stuffed toy. Then we conjured up the day. I had taken Marc to see Woodsy Owl at the park, while Don took his daughter out to lunch and on a shopping trip. Since I hadn't been there, I would never have remembered that interlude between father and daughter without the inspiration from that fifty-nine-cent toy.

Our memories, however pleasant, were not always able to stave off the feelings of loss and loneliness during the depression phase. Memories were in the past, and the sadness was in the present and the future. At the beginning of our loss I had replaced Don's presence with my mother's. Knowing that company did help, I planned to fill the emptiness during another important time—our twelfth anniversary, May 9. The day wouldn't be important for the children, but if it was a rotten day for me, my mood would influence theirs. I asked my friend Susan to come from Washington, D.C., to spend the weekend with us. Susan had been my maid of honor at our wedding, but I hadn't seen her for years. She had met Marc only once and had never seen Lara. The renewal of our friendship turned out to be one of the good things that came out of the tragedy of Don's death, and the children were delighted to have a visitor who brought them space ice cream from the National Air and Space Museum.

On the afternoon of my anniversary I dragged out the wedding photo album, so Susan and I could reminisce and help the children understand the significance of the day. Then I hired a baby-sitter and made dinner reservations at a trendy Italian restaurant that had been one of Don's favorite eating spots. I had been unable to face returning there since Don's death. Susan's presence gave me the necessary courage, but I don't remember what we had to eat that night. We polished off the bottle of wine I'd carefully chosen for the occasion.

To catch up on our years of separation, we spent the rest of her visit in long hours of talk on the back porch as the children napped or played. Susan was a single, professional woman, and I had always imagined her returning home from work after a satisfying day, stretching out on a velvet sofa in a slinky negligee to read a good book while sipping wine. In turn, she told me, she had imagined me as a superwife and mother surrounded by adorable children and adoring husband. We both laughed when we shared these visions of one another.

"I don't work well, being single," I confessed to her. Reality didn't quite match the fantasy. "I've got too much to do, taking care of this estate! And I miss sex. I was meant to be married. The next time he will have to be someone totally different from Don," I joked. "I want someone with no brains, all physical, a blond-haired, blue-eyed strongman."

We took the kids for a walk around the block. As we passed a house down the street, we noticed a muscular, blond young man in a tight-fitting "Lawn Care" T-shirt mowing the neighbor's lawn. Susan glanced at me and, with lifted eyebrow, said, "I think you need some lawn care."

After Susan left, the void gaped even wider. We had no more plans for six weeks and six weekends, until it was time to meet my parents for our postponed vacation at Disney World. Then summer would be coming and school would be out. I would lose even the little relief time I had when the children were in school.

I had been sleeping fitfully, and I always seemed to be struggling. During the day I felt the loneliness more because it seemed to stretch out endlessly into the future. Suddenly the companionship of the children was not enough, and I felt I would be alone for the rest of my life. Four months had passed, and my armor against depression slowly crumbled. I put away the sympathy cards. The mantel looked bare without them. Life looked bare without him.

For the first time since Don died I lost track of how the children were doing. Oh, I knew that neither one was suffering from the extremes of depression. Their behavior wasn't any more aggressive or withdrawn than is the norm for young children becoming more independent. They did not engage in futile behavior, searching for their dead parent, as some children do. Nearly every day Lara told me she missed her father, and sometimes she cried. Marc seemed to be pretty much on an even keel, too, and people remarked how well both children were doing. I thought they were, too. Maybe that's why I allowed myself finally to wallow in self-pity. I began to think more about me and less about the children, entering the very state that I had feared would be most detrimental to them. Indeed, it might have if either one had been less stable. After four months of coping relatively well, I had fallen into a long, adult depression.

For some bereaved parents, the depression phase induces numbing immobility, an irresistible temptation to lie down and never get up again. When I was tempted to give up, life's little jobs kept me moving like a robot. Even if I wasn't being much of a parent, I still had to provide for my children. Unfortunately, many of the jobs of a provider were totally alien to me. Keeping our car running was essential, so I went to an auto parts store for the first time in my life. Marc and Lara waited in the car in the parking lot while I hunted for a new part for the windshield wiper. The only other woman in the store was a sales clerk who ignored me to wait on other customers, all men with grease-covered hands. I wished I could have been in the car with the kids, waiting for Don as I used to. There was a sign on the wall that said, "A woman has to work twice as hard as a man to get half as much recognition. Fortunately, it isn't hard." I told myself: if Don could do it, I can do it. But I didn't like doing it. All the same, I was proud of myself after I figured out how to change the blade and the wiper actually worked.

Shopping was more up my alley, but even that simple task could have complications that reminded me of my loss. One June day in the grocery store I spotted an old acquaintance from Marc's preschool playgroup. News, especially bad news, travels fast in a small town, so I steeled myself for the inevitable questions and casually sauntered over next to her to pick out a bag of carrots. After accepting her condolences, I finished grocery shopping and headed for the card shop. Alas, another acquaintance was in that store, and rather than face her I lurked between the scented candles and the Garfield posters until she left.

Lara helped me unpack the groceries at home. I had bought Wheat Thins for the first time since Don died. In the store I'd slipped them into the shopping cart, trying not to think about how Don had craved them last fall. Lara spotted the box before I could stash it in the cupboard. "What's that?" she asked.

"Crackers," I answered flatly.

"Can I see them?" She grew excited as I handed her the box. "Daddy likes these!" she exclaimed joyfully. So did she. We opened the box and began munching.

Eventually those empty weeks passed and I became occupied with getting us ready for our trip to Disney World. All the little preparatory details still didn't keep my mind from my loss. A couple of days before our departure I stopped by the pet store to pick up fish food made for two-week vacations. I bought several packages because we would be spending the rest of our summer at the lake with my parents after the Florida trip. The friendly salesman was curious about my large purchase, so I told him about my plans.

"All summer at a lake, huh," he said. "Your husband must like to fish. It must be nice to lead a life of leisure."

It might be nice, but I wouldn't know. That night I moved my wedding band from my left hand to my right. My husband did like to fish, but I had no husband now. With no wedding band on my ring finger, I would no longer have to bear comments about my husband from virtual strangers.

The day we finally flew to Disney World was my thirty-fifth birthday. After meeting my parents and checking into the Polynesian Village, we topped off our lunch with pieces of carrot cake. That was about as much notice as I wanted made of the occasion. Throughout the vacation I wondered if it would have been easier to go in February while I was still in shock. I thought about Don constantly, what he would have been doing with us had he been able to come. I wondered if the kids did, too.

Marc didn't complain but I could tell he missed Don, because he was without a father to do the things with him that one parent divided can't provide. Though my parents helped out, several of the park attractions could only hold two people in a seat, leaving Marc stuck riding alone. A part of him liked being independent, but another part felt left out.

On the hotel beach one afternoon there was a father swimming around carrying his son piggyback. The boy's arms hugged his father's neck. They laughed and frolicked. They could have been Don and Marc. A few times while playing in the water, Marc and Lara spontaneously chanted "Daddy," as though by merely mentioning the word to each other they could conjure up his presence. I couldn't help but remember the days when Marc refused to listen to the word at all.

On our last day of vacation I was finally able to be with Marc for a few minutes alone in the pool to take him under the waterfall. He'd begged me nearly every day to go down the waterfall slide with him, but I'd put him off with the excuse that I couldn't leave Lara alone in the water. Their grandparents aren't swimmers, but I could have left Lara poolside with them for a few minutes. I just didn't want to go down the slide myself. Marc loved the splashing waterfall and I regretted not acquiescing sooner.

The next morning at breakfast Lara finally said what I'd been thinking all along, "I sure miss my daddy." We returned to our room, packed up, and went home.

I was glad the trip was over. Not that the children hadn't had a wonderful time—who can have a lousy time at Disney World? But my mother hit the nail on the head when she called to see if we had gotten home safely. "You can feel good that you've done something for the children that Don wanted to do," she said. It was like fulfilling his last wish, and that burden, at least, was lifted.

We had only a couple of weeks at home before taking off again for our summer in Michigan. We'd never spent so much of our summer with my parents before, but I thought it would be good for the children to have the close companionship of my father, especially. He'd decided to retire partly so he and my mother could spend more time with us to help us deal with our grief and depression. We all knew he couldn't replace the children's father, but he could be a healthy influence on them. I hoped his companionship might ease their feeling that something vital is missing from their lives.

Until we left, I filled the kids' days with trips to the pool club. I knew they'd miss swimming with their friends that summer, so I tried to pack in as much time there as I could. I might have overdone it, though, because Lara remarked on the shuttle trip one day, "Daddy used to take us everywhere. Now Mommy does."

When we weren't swimming, I finally tackled the dreadful job of sorting through Don's clothes. Don's sister, Barbara, was coming east later that summer to visit her parents, and I decided to take them the things of his I didn't want. Each piece of clothing, each item he'd used, seemed invested with a sign of his struggle for life. In one of his wallets, behind his draft registration card, I found a pressed four-leaf clover I never knew he had. The label in Don's raincoat collar read, "Wear in Good Health." Emptying the pockets I found an unopened roll of Life-Savers. The kids pried the slightly stale candies apart and devoured them, reminiscing about the numerous times Daddy had bought them goodies from the machines at his office. I promised them I'd save all of their father's valuable possessions, things they might want to have themselves someday. Then, they withdrew from the scene of disarray in our bedroom, wanting no further part of the disturbing task.

I didn't blame them. Folding up the blue paint-stained workshirt brought his presence achingly close. I remembered him painting the redwood fence with Marc who was protected by a plastic garbage-bag smock. And all those beautiful suits. The celebrations he'd worn them for, even the night before our wedding. The clothes he had bought himself. The gifts. The slacks I'd helped him pick out while the kids ran between the racks. The blazer I'd always taken to the cleaners and picked up again, usually the day before some meeting. I hadn't been to the cleaners since he died. And what would I do with his glasses, his windows on the world?

After three long days, Don's clothes were ruthlessly sorted, packed, and loaded in bags into the back of our station wagon. During the trip to their grandparents' house, the children pointedly ignored the extra "baggage." I'd planned to take advantage of their first chance to visit the cemetery since the funeral, and their apathetic reaction to giving away some of their father's belongings only reinforced my determination to take them. I thought that they probably needed another chance to express their sadness with me and Don's parents.

Early in the morning the day after our arrival in Connecticut we tramped through the woods across the street from their grandparents' house to pick some blossoms for the cemetery visit. The Connecticut state flower, the mountain laurel, had been Don's favorite, and Marc and Lara each carefully chose one branch of snowy white petals to carry with them.

At the cemetery we parked outside the imposing wrought-iron gate and found our way between the rows of standing stones to the back, where all the recent stones were flush with the ground. As we moved close to Don's grave, Marc and Lara grew more subdued. I sighed with relief that Don's grave looked better than the first time I'd seen it. Don's parents had planted another of his favorite flowers, marigolds, at the foot of the grave. The warm gray stone added a chiseled beauty to the barren plot, but the solid granite mass made Don's death finally seem everlasting.

Each child placed a laural spray in a pronged, cone-shaped cemetery vase as I tearfully read them the inscription on the stone. Don's mother was softly crying, too.

"Read what it says on Daddy's stone again, Mom," Marc requested.

"Devoted husband and father of Marc and Lara," I repeated.

Lara turned and walked away at the mention of her own name, saying quietly, "I don't want to hear this."

"At least they spelled my name right," Marc said with a shrug before joining his sister in a game of tag, clambering among the upright tombstones. As the children played, I quickly took a snapshot of Don's grave to put in our family photo album. Our opportunities to visit the cemetery were so rare that I wanted the children to be able to have the picture to look at if they wished.

Back in the car Marc asked, "Why did we bury Daddy here?"

"Because he was born and raised near here," I told him. "And because this spot is close to the sea. Daddy loved the ocean."

"Will I have to be buried in Lambertville?" Marc asked. Lambertville had been his first home. We had often taken walks to the quaint old hillside cemetery at the end of our street to read the interesting historic inscriptions.

"No, you can be buried anywhere you want to," I answered. He seemed satisfied and not a bit afraid.

Our visit to the cemetery did not shake my belief that seeing Don's grave would help my children to understand and accept that their father was dead, that his body was under the ground, that he was never coming back and that it was acceptable for us to cry when we thought about all that. Fortunately, I didn't expect miracles from just one visit. Many parents are so disheartened by their children's seemingly apathetic reactions to cemetery visits that they give up after one or two tries. But apathy is also an expression of depression and sadness. Lara had confronted the concrete evidence of her father's death for as long as she could, then she'd walked away. I knew she would remember. Marc's questions afterward showed me that he was still grappling with understanding his father's death, so I was encouraged. It was not easy for any of us, but to keep them away from Don's grave would have been cruel protection.

After the visit to the cemetery, I was ready to go to Michigan to be with my parents. Although I looked forward to spending July and August at the lake, it would be rough for all of us without Don. The quiet country spot, sheltered in the woods and teeming with wildlife, had always been a healing place for me. It had also been a place that Don loved. Our bittersweet memories would be especially strong there.

Despite missing Don, I gradually relaxed. Having two other adults to whom Marc and Lara could bring their questions and hurts was a tremendous restorative. I was no longer constantly on call. Consequently, the deep depression borne in the spring slowly lifted. When the children no longer had to live with an exhausted, moping mother, they seemed to cope with their sadness and longing more openly. So did I, at least most of the time.

One July day we all went shopping for Marc's first two-wheeled bicycle. After checking out every bike shop in Traverse City, my father and I agreed with Marc's choice and we returned to the first store we had visited. Unable to contain his excitement any longer, Marc bounded out of the car and slammed the door behind him, smashing my ankle against the car frame. I cried out in pain and yelled at Marc, who became distraught because he thought that now I wouldn't buy him his bike. Grumbling, I hobbled into the shop and bought the bike.

It was an accident, but I blamed Marc anyway, marring his joy. When we got back to my parents' house and unloaded the new bike, Marc asked me to help him learn to ride it. I told him I was too tired and he'd have to wait until tomorrow. Ignoring his disappointment, I excused myself, went out to the dock, and sobbed from pain both external and internal. Every time I looked at the end of the dock, I pictured Don sitting there, fishing. How could I ever cope with raising Marc? He was missing so much having only me. Don should have been there. It wasn't fair.

Marc did learn how to ride the bike, even though he became exasperated with my inability to run along and hold him steady until he learned to balance. Daddy would have done it better.

As with adults, children's longing never completely fades. Parents are forever missed each time these young people take a new step in their growth and understanding. Each important event, each passage in their lifetimes, is another that parent and child might have shared together. We will always be sad at times, because, as Lara put it, "We used to have a big family. Now we have a small one."

THE PHASES OF GRIEF:
ACCEPTANCE

The acceptance of the death of a loved one is the final phase of the grieving process. If the bereaved are given enough time and support to work through the initial phases of grief, their anger and depression will gradually abate. How much time is different for everyone. Those who reacted to their loss with stronger denial or inhibited their expression of rage and sadness will have a harder time reaching acceptance. But eventually the conflict between wanting to hold onto lost love and needing to let it go must be resolved. As grievers detach from the deceased and develop other relationships, many feel guilty that they are rejecting the deceased. At those times both children and adults need to be reminded that their parent or spouse would have wanted them to go on living, that renewal is a tribute to love once shared.

At first, acceptance can be both elusive and fleeting. It begins with cherished moments of peace between warring emotions. Gradually, the moments lengthen until the occasional intrusions of previous phases are accepted as normal grief. Many mourners are disappointed that they are not happier once they have reached this phase, that happiness is not automatic but must be built upon the peace that acceptance brings. For acceptance is still a part of the grieving process, not the end of grief.

My children's struggle to accept their father's death began almost immediately after he died and continued in a long, sometimes erratic progression. Acceptance was, after all, the period of grief to which all other phases were leading. Even in the midst of other phases, there were times when Marc and Lara seemed to possess an amazingly mature serenity as they pondered their father's death.

One August evening at the lake my mother and Lara decided to make hot buttered popcorn, the traditional family treat for TV watching. Mom told Lara that the popcorn popper had been a gift from Lara, Marc, Mommy, and Daddy.

"Daddy's dead," Lara said quietly.

"Yes, I know," my mother said.

"Even if he is dead, we still love him," Lara continued.

"We sure do."

"And Marc and I won't die until Mommy dies," Lara said with only a little nervousness.

I joined them from the hallway where I had been listening. "That won't be for a very long, long time," I added. Then I scooped Lara up in my arms and the popcorn started popping.

That conversation reminded me of one of Lara's earliest moments of acceptance, only a month after Don died. She'd just awakened from a nap and lay in her cozy bed, a particularly secure place for Lara, clutching her tattered pink blanket. As she and I snuggled warmly, she eulogized Don with still sleepy words: "We only have one daddy in the whole wide world."

"Yes," I agreed.

"Daddy wanted to stay here forever and ever," she told me.

"Yes, but he couldn't," I reminded her.

"Because he died," she said.

I attributed those early moments of calm acceptance to the blanket of security in which I enveloped my children to soften the blow they had suffered. Over the months, we had made progress from brief flashes of acceptance to a dawning realization that we must make it our way of life. We had done it by communicating with one another, by feeling our loss and our love together, and by holding on to all those positive memories we had of our time with Don.

Friends who accepted our family as a whole, even though a part was missing, had also helped us to accept that life went on, and sometimes enjoyably so. Our closest friends, Sharon and Ken, and their children, Paul and Julie, were particularly thoughtful. Soon after Don's death, on one of those dreary winter days when spirits plunge, our two families had piled into the station wagon and driven to the Franklin Institute, a science museum in Philadelphia. Don and I had always wanted to take the children there but had never gotten around to it. What impressed Marc and Lara the most about the museum, and the only part they remembered later, was the giant walk-through model of the human heart.

"What happened to Daddy's heart?" Marc asked as we entered the first chamber.

"Nothing happened to his heart. See this tube that carries blood?" I gingerly patted the huge, blue-painted cylinder. "It goes into the lung. It broke inside Daddy's body," I explained, glancing over my shoulder to see if there were any shocked eavesdroppers nearby.

I lost track of how many times we circled through that model heart. When I was beginning to feel too much like a tired blood cell, I pulled the reluctant children away.

Lara was fading fast anyway. She climbed into Julie's portable stroller and refused to budge. I started to wheel her on to the next exhibit, but she protested.

"I want Ken to push me," she insisted. She had not been in a stroller in months. As Ken obligingly wheeled her around, she seemed to revel in her regression to a time when her own father had loved to push her along in her stroller.

As I tucked a tired Marc into bed that night, I asked, "Did you like the museum today?" We gaily recalled the day's adventures.

Still smiling, Marc snuggled down under his comforter and added, "But it's too bad Daddy couldn't go."

"Yes," I said, also smiling, "he would have enjoyed it."

Saying "he would have" with a smile became an important expression of acceptance for all of us and I was relieved when my children began to say those words. Eventually they came quite often, especially at times when the children were doing things they used to do with Don.

One such activity for Marc was playing with a construction set that his Aunt Barbara had given him. Don and Marc had spent hours together making elaborate space stations, with Don usually building what Marc engineered. "Make it look like this, Daddy," he'd direct.

One day Marc spent almost an hour by himself putting the little plastic sticks together with the plastic balls. Finally he unveiled his creation to me.

"That's great!" I complimented him. "You are getting so big to be able to make that all by yourself," I told him, pleased and amazed.

Marc beamed. "Daddy would have been proud of what I made," he said confidently.

"Yes, he certainly would have." He would have been proud of us all.

There were other times during that summer in Michigan—fishing from the pontoon boat, searching for petosky stones in the bay—when we were calmly able to say that Don would have enjoyed taking part and we would have enjoyed having him there. But when summer ended, we left the peaceful lake to go back home. My former boss, Gordon, and his wife, Benita, drove us home from the Newark Airport, so I didn't have to immediately switch gears to battle the New Jersey freeways.

It was hard to go home, to readjust to the three of us living alone in that house again. Yet we all had new things to do that fall. I had enrolled in teacher certification courses at our local college because it would require fewer courses for me to get elementary certification in New Jersey, where I already had nursery school certification, than in Michigan. That decision committed us to stay in New Jersey for another year while I took my classes.

The first semester I took two courses that met back to back one night a week. Some of my old college courses had fulfilled the requirements for art and music, but not physical education. For six weeks, I had to spend four afternoons a week doing things like jumping on trampolines and running under a parachute making a noise like a giraffe. Lara was back in preschool three mornings a week, and every afternoon for those six weeks my neighbor, Penny, cared for Lara at her day-care center. We were all relieved when the course was finished.

Still, I enjoyed my classes and looked forward to getting out and socializing with other adults, some of whom were mere kids out of high school. Others, like me, were housewives who had finally found the time to further their education, now that husbands and children were capable of taking care of themselves. The first day of class I was amused to find three fellow students who had once called me "Dr. Alderman." I had been the instructor for their introductory psychology course the year before Don died. They wondered why I wasn't teaching psychology. The fact was, my part-time position didn't pay enough to support a family, and regardless of what my students had called me in class, I only had a Master's degree, not the Ph.D. necessary to get a full-time college position. I may have been the only instructor in the history of that college who later became a student there.

Marc started first grade, another milestone, without his father. The first day of school he strutted onto the bus and hopped into a seat next to a familiar face as if he'd been a first-grader all his life. He wasn't even embarrassed by his sister yelling, "Good-bye, Marc," several times.

Marc liked school right from the start because during the first week, his new teacher gave him a book to take home for a day. He won the privilege by being the closest to pronouncing correctly the main character's long Chinese name. I hoped that meant Marc would get special treatment, a little extra warmth and attention, from his teacher that year. I had requested that he be put in a male teacher's class to provide a daily role model for him. Marc similarly enjoyed his first soccer game that September. He beamed when I said, "Daddy would have been so proud of you," even though his team lost the game.

As time passes and acceptance becomes more normal, some children's memories of their dead parent fade. Although

many surviving parents are disturbed by their children's grad-
ual loss of some memories, I took Lara's confession one September morning as an indication that she was adjusting to her
life without Don.

"What does Daddy look like?" she asked curiously.

"Don't you remember?" I chided her.

"No," she honestly admitted.

"You can go look at his pictures in your photo album
after breakfast," I suggested, then described Don's distinguishing features. "He was very big and he had black hair and brown
eyes with glasses and . . ."

"And he was nice to us," Lara ended.

"Yes, he was nice to us," I agreed. If I had been tempted
to chastise myself for allowing Lara to forget her father after I'd
promised him over his grave that I wouldn't, her last remark
stopped me cold. Her emotional memory of Don's kindness
was far more important than preserving his physical appearance for her. What she remembered was the essence of the
man.

Don's birthday was also in late September. A few weeks
before the date Lara came down with a cold she undoubtedly
caught when she started back to nursery school. Pondering my
responsibilities, she sympathized with me. "When Daddy has a
cold and Marc has a cold and I have a cold, you have to take
care of us. Aren't you lucky you only have two children and not
this many?" She held up three fingers. That must have reminded her of her own age and, in turn, her last birthday. I had
not mentioned that Don's birthday was coming up, but she was
thinking of birthdays nonetheless. "Daddy will miss his birthday," she observed.

"Yes," I agreed.

"He'll *really* miss his birthday," she said emphatically.

"Yes, but he'd miss you and Marc more," I guessed.

On the morning of Don's first birthday after his death, I
decided that the children should be told what day it was,
especially since Lara had so recently mentioned the occasion.
At breakfast I announced, "Today is Daddy's birthday."

"Are we having a cake?" Marc asked doubtfully.

"No, we have no reason to celebrate without Daddy," I answered, letting him know my feelings honestly.

"It is a sad day without Daddy," Lara agreed.

"Well, I'm never sad," Marc boasted.

Lara gently advised her brother, "Marc, it's all right to be sad when we miss someone."

Marc thought a minute. "It's even good for you," he concluded.

I wondered if Marc had been avoiding feeling sad because his recent separation from his grandfather had revived his intolerable sense of loss, but his concluding statement seemed sincere. We had celebrated Don's birthday after all, if only by expressing our acceptance of our shared loss.

Even though we were busier that fall than we had been since Don died, our acceptance was not total. It was just the beginning, and there were many times when other emotions wiped out any semblance of serenity. One day in early October I sat under the hairdryer in the kitchen, getting ready for class. I told myself that I was just going to sit there and relax, something I hadn't been doing often enough lately. Instead of feeling relaxed, though, I began to get agitated. I was staring at the Dunkin' Donuts box directly in front of me on the counter. Why was I suddenly feeling a wave of grief and longing washing over me? Then I realized that three of the bold pink letters on the box spelled *Don*. I was looking at the box, but I was seeing his name.

Lara, too, had moments when the sadness wrought by Don's death suddenly crept up on her. After dinner one night, when Marc was about to feed his scraps to the dog, he asked how long his father's pet had to live. When I answered, "Oh, another four or five years," Lara began crying hysterically as if the dog would die tomorrow. Don's death was so disturbing to her that other losses, even imaginary ones, were magnified.

Autumn had challenged her to adjust to some major changes: afternoon day care and promotion to the four-year-old nursery school class with a new and less demonstrative teacher. She was also continually growing and maturing, especially in verbal skills. This growth gave her a greater ability to understand her father's death, but not enough maturity to understand totally. She grappled hard with her loss that fall, more than she had seemed to earlier. I repeatedly overheard her playing with her dolls, making one toy say to another, "My daddy is dead." She still wished that her father was alive, and she continued to speak of him in the present rather than past tense. Apparently the one time she'd corrected herself didn't have the long-lasting significance I'd hoped. Although she could say that her father was never coming back, I didn't know if she believed it.

One day she asked if she could go to Daddy's office to write with the erasable markers on his board. When I said no, she asked, "Why?" with puzzlement. Did she think he would be there or that the people he worked with might be waiting for him to come back, too?

"Because just about everything has been moved out of Daddy's office," I answered. "Maybe someday we will get you your own board."

That seemed to satisfy her, but I worried that there were so many things about Don's death she wanted to understand but simply couldn't.

I worried about Marc for a different reason; he seemed to be almost too accepting at times. He seldom talked to me about his father unless I brought up the subject. If he was repressing all of his grief to escape the immediate pain, one day the agony would erupt somehow, and we all might have hell to pay. Then again, perhaps he really had reached acceptance.

At the end of October Marc brought home a picture he drew in school entitled "My Favorite Person." At the top of Marc's picture were three childishly written letters, M-O-M. He and I both wore big smiles. I cried after I pulled it out of his bookbag, and I silently told his teacher, "Thanks, I needed that." Yet I couldn't help but think that if Don had been alive, those three letters above the smiles would have been D-A-D. Marc told me that he did another picture to keep at school that had a third figure of his friend, Chad, in it. (After all, first-graders have to start breaking the apron strings sometime.) But his sensitive teacher had let him bring this one home.

In early November, Marc broke his arm—or rather, *rebroke* it. His arm had been twisted a month earlier by an older neighborhood boy. When two doctors had told me they didn't think it was broken, I'd believed them, especially since the swelling had gone down and Marc hadn't complained of any pain as he'd continued to use it normally. But one evening while I was at class, Marc tussled with the baby-sitter. She put him to bed and he slept through the night, but the next morning his wrist was so swollen that I couldn't get his pajamas off. We went to the hospital for x-rays. Because his arm had been broken, partially healed, and rebroken, the orthopedist insisted that Marc be put under general anesthetic to have his arm set in a cast.

It was a day of pure grit for both Marc and me. I had spent too many hours in hospitals with Don, and all those sensations of anxiety and panic came flooding back to me when I saw my son lying in a bed in the pediatric ward waiting for his evening ordeal.

I spent the whole day with him in the hospital thinking how much we all needed Don there to comfort us. Lara was scared for her brother, but she couldn't stay. I called Penny to come and get her, crying on the phone, "I don't think I can take this." Lara stayed with her until Don's parents could rush down from Connecticut.

Marc and I were scared, too—he because of needles for blood tests and anesthesia, and I because I knew too well all of the things that could go wrong during simple procedures in the hospital. I insisted on taking Marc home that evening after he woke up. I told every doctor who would listen that I didn't want to traumatize Marc by making him stay overnight in the same hospital where his father had died in the emergency room.

But nothing went wrong. In two weeks Marc was out of his cast and into an Ace bandage. He suffered very little pain, though I suffered a whole lot of fatigue from waiting on him for two weeks, dressing him, feeding him, entertaining him.

November was the tenth month since Don had died. Suddenly it seemed like a very long time; we were into double digits. When I thought about that I was struck by the emotional conviction that he wasn't coming back. There was no need to stay in the house. He wouldn't return to find us gone. *He* was gone. I decided to put the house up for sale.

Cleaning the house for showing was spirit-breaking, rather than back-breaking work. When I tried to scrub off mud spots in the entryway which I never really noticed before, they flaked off in reddish, powdery flecks. Don must have been carried on the stretcher headfirst down the three steps, spattering the wall with his blood as a kind of farewell to the home he was leaving for the last time. I scrubbed hard, but I couldn't get it all off. The next owner would just have to paint over it.

The same day I transferred the contents of Don's bathroom drawer into the cupboard below. I didn't have the energy to sort through his toiletries, but we needed the drawer space to clear off the counter. Potential buyers were impressed by neatness. Don had kept his hairbrush in that drawer, and single strands of his hair still clung to the paper liner. As I washed them down the drain, I felt bitter that twice in the same day I had found signs of him which had outlasted his physical presence for almost a year. If his blood and hair could still be around, why couldn't he?

In mid-November my parents came to stay for a few weeks. I took the opportunity to get away for a weekend, visiting Susan in Washington, D.C. It was a wonderfully relaxing time, filled with good restaurants, museums, and Kennedy Center music. When I returned home, we all had a joyous reunion with presents that I'd bought for the children at a craft fair. After things settled down Lara climbed into my lap. It was then that she asked, "When will Daddy wake up?"

I was taken aback. I didn't immediately understand her question. "What do you mean, sweetheart?" I asked.

"When will Daddy come back?"

Aha! After all, I had gone and come back. Daddy loved her as much as Mommy does, so if Mommy came back, Daddy will, too. Her logic was flawless.

"Daddy can't come back. He's dead," I explained again. "But Mommy will always come back."

"To protect us?"

"To protect you." Lara still needed a lot of reassurance that her world was secure even without her father.

Marc's seventh birthday was a few days after my getaway weekend, and Lara had turned four in early November. I kept both celebrations low-key that year: a few friends over for cake and ice cream, but no flashing cameras or elaborate entertainment. I still felt bitter that Don wasn't there to put together the big toys and blind us all with his movie camera floodlight. Marc and Lara didn't say so, but I could tell they sensed a disquieting difference, the absence of someone important, on their special day. Marc, at least, had his grandfather there to help fill the void for his seventh birthday.

My parents' visit helped us get through the beginning of the holiday season I so dreaded. I'd read or heard all sorts of advice for the widowed parent on how best to handle holidays, days which used to be occasions for joy but which had suddenly become bittersweet. My only thought was to spend them together as a family to find out what worked best for all of us.

Throughout the year we had taken each important date as best we could. I tried to enjoy Mother's Day because the children were excited about their carefully handmade gifts and cards. No matter how much fuss anyone else made over me, though, I sorely missed the tender attention from Don, and especially so on my birthday. On Father's Day we sent flowers to the cemetery and presents to the children's two grandfathers.

I hoped the bustle and frenzy of Thanksgiving and Christmas would sweep me into the spirit of things for the sake of the children. It wasn't easy, and we broke with tradition for both holidays. On Thanksgiving we went out to dinner for the first time. I made little blank paper booklets for each of the children to color in between courses. Not only did that allow the adults to have a peaceful meal, but it gave the children a keepsake of our Thanksgiving in a restaurant. It was a pleasant day and different. It just didn't seem like Thanksgiving, which was probably best for us all. The next year, we could switch to turkey at Grandma's or maybe I'd go back to fixin' the trimmin's.

It wasn't only the actual holidays that I dreaded so

much, for the time leading up to each holiday is usually so full of anticipation. Without Don to help us shop for gifts, decorate the house, and plan our celebrations, those preparations seemed like a lot of work for nothing.

Yes, the kids were both excited about the holidays. Marc had lapses in his self-control during the whole holiday season, continually annoying me with mildly rebellious behavior and hyperactivity. I wished that he could open up, talk about Don, and admit that he missed him, and was concerned that that misbehavior might be a symptom of his repression of grief. Bringing up my own feelings about Don whenever I could only did so much for Marc, but I didn't know what else to do, except to wait patiently. Ultimately his acceptance would have to come from within.

Ironically, Lara seemed to be making quantum leaps toward accepting the finality of Don's death. "Only when you play, a dead person can come alive," she informed me in early December. "When you're really dead, you're dead forever. You can never wake up again."

Yet as I drove home after my last class before Christmas, I could almost hear Don describing his ride on the same road after work the year before. "The Christmas lights along the way home are so beautiful, Linda. I wish you could see them."

I was glad when Christmas was upon us, because that meant it would soon be over. At least I could be thankful that we planned to spend the holiday with my parents in their new home in northern Michigan. The night before our trip west I took the kids out for fast food. As we passed houses all decorated with gaily colored lights, I said to the kids, "Look out the window. It's your last chance to see the Christmas lights of Flemington." Sadness engulfed me as I realized what I'd said. Next year we would be moved. It really was our last chance to see these lights. We would miss our home and the star which had once shone so brightly in the east for us.

To the children, our move was a long way off yet. They were delighted to fly to their first Christmas at the lake, where sledding down snowbanks was almost as much fun as opening presents. Although I understood that many families find comfort in carrying on old traditions after a parent's death, I felt that building new traditions for our family would help us accept that our lives had forever changed. The new environment took away some of the sting of longing for Christmases past. At the lake we could still reminisce and still miss Don, but we could also still celebrate. Yet the quality of our rejoicing had changed, too; our joy had lost some of its innocence. We celebrated us, our closeness, and our survival.

As relieved as I was that our first holiday season without Don had been dutifully marked and passed, I couldn't let down my guard and jump back into our stabilizing routine quite yet. Back at home, one more ordeal loomed in early January: the first anniversary of Don's death. When I awoke on the eighth of January, I told myself that this was just another day, and I resolved to hold on to that thought. The children carried on as usual, unaware of the significance of the date. I was holding up pretty well—so well that by late afternoon I felt ready to tackle one of those many "male" jobs that could shake my self-confidence. The garage door remote control wasn't working, and changing the battery (Marc's suggestion) didn't work. So the three of us drove to the nearby Sears catalogue store to order a new button. In the car I finally mentioned to the kids, "You know, one year ago today Daddy died."

"I miss him," Lara said.

"So do I," I agreed.

"Well, I don't," Marc said stoically. "I'm too busy."

Swallowing my discouragement over his persistent repression, I tried once more to break through his little-boy macho. "It's good to keep busy when you are sad, Marc. I do that, too. But it's all right to miss Daddy. He'd want us to think about him."

Marc just glared at me as though he resented me for bringing the whole subject up, and we drove the rest of the way in silence. At the store the kids wandered around among the refrigerators and televisions while I was waited on by a saleswoman. She searched the catalogue for the right button, but she was obviously confused. A man standing next to me gave me some free advice while he waited to pick up his order.

"I wouldn't do that if I were you. I used to work for Sears service department, so I know. Everyone makes the same mistake. It won't do any good to order a new remote control if the radio transmitter isn't working. Those things must cost over thirty dollars. Do you live near a Sears retail store?"

"No. I live right here in Flemington." If I lived near a retail store, I'd have gone there. A feeling of panic welled up in my chest as the man continued, oblivious to my labored breathing. Somehow I was losing control of the situation.

"Well, there's a lever to disconnect the whole unit from the wall. Take it off and carry it yourself to a service center. They'll fix it for less than if they have to make a service call." And I'd only have to make two forty-mile round trips, if I could get the thing off the wall.

A young salesman behind the counter had another theory. "Did you take apart the remote control and clean it up? Sometimes they get oil or dirt in them."

"No. I don't even know how to take this apart." I tugged at the offending button as tears of exasperation flooded my eyes. The guy didn't offer any further advice on how to dissect the button either. I focused on the woman. "Just write down the catalogue number. I'll order by phone," I instructed her.

"They're a big help, aren't they? Men!" she said as she handed me the number.

I grabbed the paper and fled, literally dragging the children with me. Safely back in the car I sobbed and then yelled at the kids when they asked me what was the matter.

Don't lose control, Linda, I told myself. Not until you get back home. I plastered on a twisted smile and drove to the mall. Marc got a haircut and we all played video games in the arcade before eating at McDonald's, all an attempt to be festive.

By the time I pulled into our driveway, my emotional turmoil had subsided. I let the kids into the house, opened the garage door by hand, and parked the car in the garage. As I came inside, Marc and Lara stood on either side of the top of the three steps leading to the living room, smiling sweetly. Unbeknownst to me, they had cooked up a practical joke. Marc smacked me sharply with the flat of his hand against the top of my head, and Lara swung in imitation as I started up the stairs.

Immediately I screamed, "How can you do that to me,

today of all days!" Surprised by my anger, neither child had an answer. Marc, the obvious instigator, looked shocked at his own behavior. If I'd been calm enough to assess the situation, I might have realized that he hadn't intended to hit me so hard. I might also have surmised that his grief had finally erupted in a brief but violent rage directed toward me because I had reminded him of the day his father died.

But I was far from calm, and all I wanted to do was escape from these two malicious children. I continued upstairs and locked myself in my room until their bedtime. I tucked them in curtly with no kisses or hugs and holed up alone again in my room. It was a lot harder to get obedience and respect as a single parent, I had discovered, because there was no other parent to reinforce my standards. Yet my children's unkindness had hurt me more than their blows. So much for making it through January 8.

Strangely, after that episode Marc began to mention Don more and in ways that gave me some hope he finally might be wrestling with acceptance. One morning soon after the "anniversary," Marc asked questions that made the cereal stick in my throat.

"How does Daddy's body turn into a skeleton, Mom?"

"The skin and muscles sort of dry out and flake off, Marc. They'll be absorbed by the earth," I explained poetically. I couldn't bring myself to say the word *rot*.

"Is Daddy a skeleton yet?" Marc persisted.

"I don't know. I don't know how long it takes," I answered uneasily. I have to admit that I had ghoulishly wondered that myself.

"What will happen to his clothes?"

"I guess his clothes will still be there on his skeleton," I judged, maybe incorrectly. Which rots faster, the human body or cloth? I was suddenly piqued that Don's clothes might last longer than he did. But it heartened me that Marc was able to talk about the decomposition of Don's body. Though ghoulish, it was a topic that forced us to move closer to accepting reality.

That winter Marc seemed to grow more comfortable when speaking about his father, as he had been right after Don's death. He even told me quite casually one day that he'd had a dream in which Don appeared briefly. The apparition was a bit vague, but neither frightening nor realistic, and not very significant to Marc either.

Marc's behavior gradually changed from unbearable to exemplary, and he was no longer willful and uncooperative as he had been during the holidays. His recovery may have been partly due to the passing of the season, but I also attributed some of his good humor to a growing acceptance. He seemed to be more like his old self, engagingly open about his feelings, whether they were loving or angry.

It was the time of year when winter doldrums were setting in and the movie industry was counting on that mood to draw crowds to the heavily advertised film, *Dark Crystal*. Every time I watched the commercial for the movie, I regretted that Don had missed another event he would have enjoyed immensely. Every time Lara watched the same commercial she warned, "I'm not going to see that. It's too scary!"

Marc, of course, was itching to see the movie. "Can we go see *Dark Crystal*?" he begged each time the promo aired.

When the movie came to our local theater, I was forced to make a decision. "No, Lara is too scared to go and her feelings would be hurt if we left her home." Then Marc was hurt that I chose to honor Lara's feelings over his desire for some good fun. "I wish Daddy were still alive!" he said angrily. "Then he could take me to the movies and you could stay home with Lara, like we used to!"

I wished that, too, but I was encouraged that Marc's disappointment at missing the movie didn't start another cycle of silence and resistance, as it might have a few months earlier. Maybe he was placated when I took him and his sister to see *Peter Pan* as a compromise.

I was reassured further when I overheard Marc on the phone with a classmate one Saturday in late January. "Ryan, can you come over and play?" he asked rather shyly. " 'Cause, you know, it's, uh, kind of boring without a father."

A sure sign of acceptance to me was when the children calmly began to share their loss with their friends. Some children whose fathers or mothers have died feel so different from other children that they hide the parent's death from their playmates. Their school companions, in turn, may shun them in order to avoid the embarrassment of not knowing what to say and to deny their own fears that what happened to someone else's parent could happen to theirs.

Bereaved children may feel different, even from friends whose parents are divorced. Children of divorced couples still have two parents, no matter how seldom they see the absent one. Even with today's high divorce rate, the nuclear family, myth or not, is still considered to be the norm. A family is supposed to consist of a mother, a father, a son, and a daughter, an ideal we had achieved, only to lose.

Curiously, a year earlier Marc had seemed to feel freer to talk about his loss with other children than in recent months. I remembered one Saturday afternoon the previous spring when Marc and his friend, Chad, had been busy in our playroom.

"I'm going to play baseball with my dad today," Chad had said.

"We don't have a daddy," Marc had told Chad, even though Marc knew that his friend knew it.

"I know," Chad had answered sympathetically.

Lara had chirped up from her doll corner, "Our daddy died."

A few minutes later Chad had tired of play. "I'm going home now," he'd politely told Marc.

"Why?" Marc had asked, puzzled.

"I just want to," Chad had insisted.

"But why?" Marc had demanded. What was there better to do than play with a friend on Saturday afternoon?

"I want to see my dad. I haven't seen him for the whole week!" Chad's father traveled for his business.

Marc had softly closed the front door behind his friend and, turning to me, said, "Well, I can't see mine for the rest of my life!"

Perhaps it had been easier for Marc to talk to his friends about the death of his father when he was younger, a kindergartener who, like most kids that age, was still engagingly uninhibited. Perhaps it had taken him a few months in first grade to feel comfortable confiding in his new classmates. After the reality of his father's death had hit him, he'd needed time to begin to accept his loss before he could confide in his friends again.

Lara, at least, had continued to talk openly about Don as much as a four-year-old could. One winter day she was watching Marc play checkers. "Daddy plays checkers with me sometimes. He helps me build towers, but they always fall down," she sighed.

A few days later when she came down with the flu, her spirits plummeted. As we sat cuddled together on Don's favorite chair, she stared at our family portrait on the opposite wall. "If Daddy was here, he would fix me," she moaned.

I took her into the kitchen to spoon-feed her some peaches. Still thinking of Don, she smiled weakly and said, "That's Daddy's favorite fruit. He shared his with me. He always takes out the pit." Unfortunately, neither he nor I had been able to protect her and her brother from life's pits.

In the beginning of March, Marc found a dead rabbit on the wooded path leading to Chad's house. From its markings I recognized it as the one which had magically appeared in our yard during Lara's last birthday party before Don died. Some lout of a hunter was a lousy shot and had only wounded the animal. It must have hopped back to the woods and bled to death. Marc raced into the house in a state of shock. He thought it was the Easter bunny: another dead dream. Who gave that hunter the right to destroy my children's dreams, I thought angrily, not to mention my memories?

Although I had begun to accept Don's death, I still felt so unnaturally alone. My second semester of college would soon be over, putting an end to the one night a week of adult companionship. I'd been on my own long enough to prove to myself I could do it, and increasingly weary of doing it all alone, I finally was willing to accept more help. Living close to my parents would bring relief from my burdens and more company for us than mere memories could provide. I eagerly anticipated the change that our move to Michigan would bring. Anything different would have to be better.

Having real estate agents bring prospective buyers to tromp through our house, each one mentally making it theirs for a few minutes, upset us all. The kids hated it because of the frenzy of clean-up before each appointment and because it reminded them that they would soon be leaving their friends. I hated it because each prospective buyer found something to criticize about my beloved house. Some wanted to change the wallpaper or kitchen cabinets. One actually wanted to raise the roof on the master bedroom.

One couple brought their parents along for a second look. Usually I tried to stay in the background when people looked at the house, letting the agent handle everything. The kids and I would perch on the sofa and read a book, acting like the model family. This time, though, the father buttonholed me for questioning.

"Why are you selling the house?" he asked suspiciously.

He could easily have asked the agent that question and she could have told him. "Because my husband died and the house is too much for me to take care of alone," I told him.

"Oh, I'm sorry. What did he die of?" he asked.

That is really none of your business, I thought. "Cancer," I answered curtly.

"Oh, where did he die? In the hospital?"

That was enough. "No, actually he dropped dead right there on the kitchen floor." I smiled.

The man immediately excused himself and went to get his daughter and son-in-law. They never made an offer on the house. I didn't want them living there anyway. After that I also tried to arrange showings for the times when the children were at school.

Strangely, as a part of our lives seemed to be drawing to a close that spring, I was called upon to make a new beginning, one that provided companionship and nourished my acceptance. One day when I picked Lara up at nursery school, her teacher asked to talk to me privately. Uh-oh, I thought, what's wrong with Lara?

But she didn't want to talk about Lara. She wanted to discuss another mother whose husband had died of a heart attack at a Christmas party a few months earlier. "She needs help. Is there anywhere for her to go to get it?"

"No," I answered. "But I'll call her." I still needed help,

too, and I began to think how comforting it would be to get a support group going for widowed parents. I called the woman and we got together one evening. A rapport developed between us so quickly that we decided to see if we could find other widows to join us. My family doctor and word of mouth turned up six widows and one widower who was a social worker. One woman's husband had committed suicide seven years earlier, but she still needed help. Another woman with several children was engaged to marry the bachelor next door, but she still came. We met at each other's houses every other week, just to talk. I quickly discovered the healing power of talk, especially when the listeners are people with a shared hurt. I was disappointed that I would soon be leaving the group when I moved to Michigan.

I wasn't the only one who began sharing my loss with others that spring. Lara was gaining a little more confidence at preschool, and I was pleased when she asked if she could invite a classmate to lunch after school one day. In the car the girls traded secrets. Lara's was a big one.

"My daddy died," she told Wendy. When Wendy was silent, Lara insisted, "He did. He really did."

Wendy yelled to me in the front seat for confirmation. "Did Lara's daddy die?"

"Yes." I answered simply. I wanted Lara to handle her tale her own way.

She elaborated in detail to impress Wendy with the truth. "He had something growing inside him that wasn't supposed to be. He got a hole in his tube. All his blood come out of his mouth and nose."

"That's too bad," Wendy said, expressing her sympathy.

"Yes, he died," Lara repeated.

"No, I mean it's too bad that you are sad," Wendy corrected. She was rightly more concerned about how Lara felt than about a strange man's death.

"Yeah, now I don't have a daddy. I miss him," Lara freely admitted, dry-eyed. Then the girls changed the subject, talking about their Strawberry Shortcake doll collections. Just as Marc had begun to talk about his loss with his friends earlier, now Lara was able to do so with her friends. And if their friends could accept my two beautiful children without a father, then they could accept themselves.

Acceptance is an uneven path, and for growing children, one riddled with confrontations, some forcing struggles with painful reality, others leading to mature insight. In May Lara graduated from nursery school and Marc and I went to watch her receive her diploma. Dressed in her finery, Lara reveled in her glory until we were back at home and she had to get ready for bed. Realizing that she would not be seeing her teachers any more, she cried, first because we nearly couldn't find the doll she wanted to cuddle, then because she'd miss her teachers, and finally because she missed Daddy.

"Daddy didn't even get to see my first teachers," she complained as I tucked her in.

"No, he didn't get to see you in school this year either. But he would have been proud of the way you've grown," I complimented her.

"Does he know that I'm bigger?" she asked.

"No. When people are dead they can't know about us anymore," I answered, trying as usual to be concrete with her questions.

"Maybe he can dream what I've been doing, like he's sleeping," she imagined.

"I don't think so. He's not asleep," I emphasized. I have never linked death with sleep for my children, an association which could cause them to fear closing their eyes in their beds at night.

"Well, I can pretend that he can imagine how big I am," she continued wistfully. "Maybe he can."

I wondered myself about Don's life after death and questioned whether we were still as much a part of him as he was of us here on earth. "Well, we really don't know what happens to people after they die. Maybe somehow he knows all about us. I know that if he could, he would be proud of you," I repeated.

"What if I didn't have Grandma and Granddad and my mommy died?" she asked again.

"I'm not going to die now, Lara. I'm healthy. I'll take

care of you," I promised. "And anyway, you do have Grandma and Granddad."

"But they are old," she protested.

My mother would not have appreciated that, I thought. "But they are not going to die yet either. They will get older before they die."

Lara nodded wisely. "People don't die before they get very old, but Daddy wasn't old enough to die." She understood with evident relief that her father's death was the inexplicable exception to the rule.

A few weeks after Lara's graduation we sold our house to a couple with two boys just the right age to be playmates for Penny's children next door. I was genuinely pleased that our home would still be filled with the laughter of youngsters. We spent the rest of the summer attending to unfinished business— arranging for our move, packing, and saying a series of good- byes. I suspected that it would be a long time before we came back to the East Coast, maybe never. Don's parents also had their house on the market so they could relocate closer to their daughter, Barbara. After they moved, there would be no com- pelling reason for us to travel east. Besides our friends, the only thing left there would be Don's grave.

Our first important farewell was a trip to Connecticut in June. The children had gone back to the cemetery only once more that year, so I'd been surprised when Lara commented out of the blue a few months earlier, "I miss Daddy. At least we planted the flowers."

"What flowers?" I had no idea what she was talking about.

"You know," she'd struggled to explain, "the ones at the synogod, at that place where Daddy's thing is."

"Do you mean the cemetery?"

"Yes," she'd exclaimed, happy to be understood. "Where Daddy's stone is!"

I'd promised her we could take more flowers to the cemetery when we next visited Don's parents, and we did indeed bring more to Don's grave for Father's Day. All three of us were aware we would soon be leaving the East Coast, so our last visit to Don's burial place was bittersweet.

Standing by his grave, I spoke to the children through tears. "We may not be back for a while, so maybe we'd better say good-bye." I knelt in front of the stone, placed a kiss on my fingertips, and rubbed them over Don's name. "Good-bye, Don I love you," I whispered.

Marc sniffled. "Good-bye, Daddy. I love you. Daddy would have been proud of me and my report card, wouldn't he, Mommy?"

"Yes, he certainly would have!" I hugged Marc and Lara. And Lara—Lara who is usually so talkative—just stood and sobbed. She sobbed all the way back to Don's parents' house.

Perhaps we could have avoided all those tears by simply skipping the visit to the cemetery. But then we would have lost an important opportunity to share some deep feelings together. I didn't want my children to feel guilty about leaving their father behind, either, and they might have without a proper good-bye.

My thirty-sixth birthday was a few days after Father's Day. Back home we all made wishes on the candles and blew them out together.

"What did you wish, Mom?" Lara asked.

"We can't tell," Marc cautioned, "or the wish won't come true."

Unfazed by her brother's warning, Lara couldn't keep her secret. "I wished that I wouldn't die when I'm a Mommy," she said excitedly.

I wished that my children's wishes could be more innocent.

Our summer passed in long hours of child's play alternating with packing. The closing on our house was scheduled for the end of August so that we could get moved in time for the children to start school in Michigan. Our one respite from the endless drudgery of packing everything we owned into boxes and cartons was a trip just before the Fourth of July to California to spend the holiday with Aunt Barbara, Uncle Mel, and cousins Andy and Tammy. Marc and Lara had a ball romping in the pool with their older cousins, while Barbara and I steeped in the hot tub. The kids were sorry to leave California, and the first night back Marc lay crying in his bed when I went to tuck him in.

"I miss Aunt Barbara and Uncle Mel and Andy and Tammy," he told me when I asked what was wrong.

It was so unusual for him to cry for people he knew he would surely see again that I had to ask, "Do you miss Daddy, too?" Marc was sobbing so hard that he could only nod. "I miss him, too, Marc, but I am here and I love you." I tried to comfort him, but he cried himself to sleep.

Perhaps, as we said our farewells and packed our belongings, it was the overwhelming feeling of the end of one part of our lives, or maybe it was a natural time when each of us had begun to accept our loss, but for whatever reason, we started thinking about death in new ways. Each of us—Lara, Marc, and myself—had begun to show a heightened interest in a spiritual concept of death, something I first noticed after we paid a farewell visit to an old college friend, Karen, her daughter, Emily, and Karen's younger sons. As we ate dinner back home that evening, Lara told me thoughtfully, "Emily said that Daddy is in heaven." Emily was Marc's age, and Lara obviously respected her wisdom.

"Some people believe that people's spirits go to heaven after they die," I commented noncommittally.

"Do you?" she cornered me.

I thought for a moment, unsure of my own beliefs. Pulled between wanting to believe and refusing to, I had to answer the only way I knew how, honestly. "I don't know. No one knows for sure what happens to people after they die."

Marc, the inheritor of his father's logic, added, "That's because no one's ever lived to tell about it."

It was not the first time my children had mentioned spiritual concerns to me, but they had begun expressing such thoughts more frequently. The questions Marc and Lara asked put me in a quandary. I didn't want to deny them the consolation they might find from conventional Christian beliefs in an afterlife or to tell them what they ought or ought not to believe. But I was in the midst of a crisis in my own faith. My anger at God for letting Don die had not completely faded, and I hadn't the time or energy to sort out what I believed about an afterlife. My spiritual state was more like a vague envy of people whose faith was strong or simple enough to enable them to go on believing, in this world of suffering.

Yet even parents with deep faith and strong beliefs can be in as much of a quandary as I was when faced with the death of a parent. Surviving parents are often puzzled by how to present their spiritual concepts of death to a bereaved child. One confused woman friend told me that she'd explained to her daughter, "Jesus took Daddy to heaven to be with God."

The child had responded with dismay and anger, asking, 'If Jesus had room for Daddy, why doesn't he have room for me?''

Marc and Lara were raised rather ecumenically, with both Jewish and Christian backgrounds. Their spiritual concept of death had started to form on the night Don died, with my spur-of-the-moment inspiration that Daddy's spirit was the feeling of his love all around us which would be with us always. Over the months since then, I'd used my instinct and common sense to fumble my way through their religious questions. Later, when I would return to the solace of the church of my youth, my desire to assure the children of God's love would feed their already growing understanding of a concept of everlasting life. I only wish that I had discovered Earl Grollman's book, *Talking About Death: A Dialogue Between Parent and Child,* and Janette Klopfenstein's Christian-oriented book, *Tell Me About Death, Mommy,* earlier. Since religion is as personal as death, I can only share my thoughts and our experience for parents and other caring adults to consider.

Erna Furman warns that young children who have not yet developed the capacity to think abstractly may be so confused by religious or philosophical explanations of death that they may distort an idea that adults find comforting into something very frightening. In retrospect, I am very glad that I never told Marc and Lara that Jesus or God took Daddy to heaven when they asked, "Why did Daddy die?"

Some religious parents may be tempted to use that quick answer in the same way that adults used to tell children that babies were delivered by storks or found under a leaf in a cabbage patch. Almost everyone recognizes now that evading the truth about the facts of life with simple stories cheats the child out of the chance to develop a healthy outlook on physical love. Unfortunately, adults do not always recognize that oversimplified religious explanations of death may cheat the child out of developing a healthy spiritual love. This may be even more damaging, because although children seldom develop unreasonable fears of storks or cabbages, they can come to fear God or Jesus.

Rabbi Earl Grollman, a sensitive religious leader and noted expert on communicating with children about death, cautions that a child who attributes the cause of his or her parent's death to God may resent God for taking the much-loved and needed parent away. That child may also reason logically that if God took a parent out of love, then maybe God will take the child next, and soon. After all, the child has also been told, "God loves you."

Rarely, a child in the depression phase of grief may take matters into his or her own hands. If a child says, "I want to be in heaven with Daddy [or Mommy]," there may be a danger of suicide, in which case professional counseling is advisable.

Bereaved children who ask why their parent died need to be told the physical cause of death, no matter how unpleasant it may be for the surviving parent to explain. By explaining the cause of death as a car accident or heart failure rather than invoking the intervention of God, children may be better able to grasp the idea that God is standing by to help us with love, in good times and in bad. Disease and accidents happen in our imperfect world. I believe that, when these happen, God steps in to give support and love. I also believe that children can accept that order of things without resentment and fear. At least I believe that now. At the time that Don died, I did not tell Marc and Lara that his spirit was with God or in heaven, not because I wanted to preserve their positive feelings for religion, but because I couldn't believe it myself.

Adults often say "It was God's will," to console surviving loved ones after a death. Very few children, experiencing their personal loss from their naturally egocentric perspective, find these words comforting. As an adult, I can understand that God's plan may never be clear to me in life and that good can grow from tragedy. Even so, I was not on speaking terms with God for a long time after Don died. It was only after months of soul-searching that I stopped blaming God for Don's cancer. When I finally felt a need to be rid of the anger that was denying me spiritual comfort, I was able to share with Marc and Lara an uplifting belief in Don's heavenly afterlife with God and in God's love for us. And that, I believe, is "God's will."

By the summer of our move to Michigan, Marc and Lara had already more or less reached that belief before me, being so informed by some of their little friends: ". . . and a little child shall lead them" (Isaiah 11:6).

The seeds of their belief had been planted not very long after Don died. Lara had listened intently one day as Marc had told me, "Brian said that God makes people alive again in heaven. He changes them into angels. He said I can see my daddy again when I die. I hope it's true."

Trying to avoid the whole subject at that time, I'd only said, "Lots of people beleive that it is true. Why did Brian tell you that? Did he know that Daddy died?"

Impatiently Marc had answered, "I told him!"

"I'm glad you have a friend you can talk to," I'd said, closing the subject.

We'd also had another "religious" discussion around the time of Don's birthday. As the three of us were eating breakfast one morning, Marc had plucked a white dog hair off his toast. It belonged to Saskia, the dog we had inherited from Don, much to my dismay. She was definitely man's best friend, not woman's. Marc knew that she was born before he was, and he sometimes worried that she'd die soon.

"Will Daddy see Saskia in heaven?" Marc had wondered.

"I don't know." With such questions of immortality coming up regularly, I was beginning to see that maybe I didn't have all the answers. I had never been afraid to tell my children that I didn't know the answers to their questions. I wanted them to understand that we never stop learning. Deep down inside, I had hoped that honesty might allow them the freedom and comfort of belief that I was still denying myself.

"What if Daddy's in heaven?" Lara had asked sadly. "I'll miss him." She'd preferred to have his spirit closer to her.

"I'll miss him, too, Lara," I'd agreed. "But we already miss him now."

As we prepared to move, I found most of my spiritual comfort from being in the great outdoors. The children and I spent innumerable hours in our backyard. Our favorite pastime was space travel in the apple tree, an imaginary trip that Don's friend, Les, had initiated with Marc before Don died. We'd had lots of time to develop and refine the game. As astronauts have testified, space travel can be a spiritual experience, and even our imaginary flight from our perches above the ground and closer to the heavens seemed to bring us grace.

Our second favorite pastime was swinging, another skyward ride. On one bright and sunny summer day I took a break from packing. Lara and I were alone in our cozy backyard, isolated from the others by overgrown shrubbery. I pushed her on her swing, watching her delight in the feeling of freedom children enjoy in defying gravity. Her long blond hair swished back, tickling my face with each push. As she reached high into the air she said, "Daddy's up there in the sky above those clouds, isn't he?"

"Well, I'm not sure heaven is just above those clouds," I said, amazed at myself for agreeing with Lara that Don could be in heaven. "No one really knows for sure where heaven is. People like to imagine that heaven is above the clouds," I explained.

"It's really underground, because I know that Daddy is underground. He's in a coffin, isn't he?" It was Lara's turn to grapple with the separation of body and spirit as Marc had when we compared Don to Obi-wan Kenobi.

"Yes, his body is in a coffin. But his spirit isn't," I emphasized. "Some people believe that a person's spirit goes to heaven."

"Daddy's spirit is with us," she decided. Like me, she still needed him nearby. "I wish Daddy were alive. It's more fun to be alive than to be dead. Do you remember how much fun we had when Daddy used to take us to the playground?"

"Yes, I remember, and I'm glad you do too," I said.

"Sometimes at night when I go to bed, I imagine that Daddy is in the ground under our house," she confided.

"Does that make you feel good to imagine that he is close by?" I asked.

"Yes," she answered with contentment, "I like to imagine that he is under our house."

Whether the spiritual concepts the children developed by themselves added to, or resulted from, accepting their father's death, I will never know. Both may be true. I do know that acceptance did come from them, as an intermittent yet dominant part of their journey through grief. Life is never again quite so easy for mourning children, but they learn to live with longing.

One day before everything was packed up Lara took her best friend, Julie, on a tour of Don's study. Julie pointed to the old fuzzy knickknack troll and asked curiously, "What's that?"

"It's my daddy's, but he isn't here," Lara said.

"I know, he's dead." Julie hadn't forgotten. "Why did he die?" she asked Lara.

Lara thought for a moment before answering matter-of-factly, "He had a broken heart."

All four of us had had broken hearts, but with time, each other's support, and the help of all our friends, those hearts mended. Our hearts keep on beating steadily in rhythm together even though they will always carry scars. Our hearts are strong, perhaps stronger now than ever before.

*H*OW OTHER ADULTS CAN HELP

One summer day I took Marc and Lara to a story hour at a different library. My children blended right in with the other tykes, who were listening raptly to the librarian recite a nursery rhyme about cats. One little girl piped up, "My father hates cats."

The librarian was unruffled. "Well, that's all right. Some people aren't fond of cats. Some people may like other animals instead."

Another little girl chimed in, "We used to have a cat, but it died."

Still unruffled, the librarian had a consoling answer. "That's all right. Cats sometimes die when they get very old."

Marc, however, wasn't about to miss the chance for one-upmanship. "My father died, and he wasn't very old," he calmly announced.

This time the librarian was ruffled. Fighting to maintain her composure, she raced on, "Well, that's all right. That happens sometimes. Now let's read our story!"

Well, that's not all right, I thought. Children need sympathy as much as adults do to work through the mourning process. And the adults in each bereaved child's life who are willing to give such sympathy can—if only they know how. As I struggled to help my children heal, I realized that other adults who would like to help were as much at a loss as I was. My children's grandparents were unfailing in their continuous expressions of love and support for us all. Yet I know there were times when they fell back on old-fashioned common sense and a prayer when answering some of their grandchildren's questions. Loving relatives and friends, as well as teachers, likewise tried their best. In the years since their father died Marc and Lara have encountered many people with varying degrees of training who played helping roles in their lives—clergy, religious teachers, physicians, nurses, hospice volunteers, art therapists, and librarians, among others. Psychologists, social workers, and even funeral-home directors are other professionals who are frequently faced with counseling bereaved children. What these people have in common with the surviving parent is that all are dismally prepared to help bereaved children. Because parental death is less common than divorce and other types of loss, the problems of bereaved children are less widely discussed, leaving most adults with little experience helping a child mourn. Unfortunately, when adults do take the time to learn about childhood bereavement, their initiative may well be motivated by the inadequacy they feel during an unexpected encounter with a mourning child.

Even well-prepared teachers such as myself, trained to teach everything from the life cycle of an apple tree to rules for fire safety and prevention, are often totally unprepared when a young student mentions death, especially his or her personal experience with death. My first encounter with a young child's bereavement was before Marc and Lara were born, the first year I taught nursery school. Fresh out of college, I had been teaching a class of three-year-old children for *five* months. It was early June and nearing the end of the school year. One of our last projects was to make plaster of paris paperweights decorated with tiny stones that we had collected on a nature walk. I explained to my eighteen white-speckled children that tomorrow we would wrap up their dried plaster creations for them to give to their fathers on Father's Day. One quiet little girl looked up at me and announced reticently, "I don't have a father. They took him away in an ambulance."

My mouth dropped open in shock and, yes, embarrassment. Reacting on the spur of the moment, without much experience to guide me, I fumbled to change the subject as soon as possible. "Well, you can give it to your grandfather or maybe an uncle," I suggested hopefully. "Now does anyone else need any help?"

The little girl, of course, was the one who needed help. And so did I. Looking back, I realize that I probably could have handled just about any other problem better than I handled the young girl's experience with death. I'd known that I would have students whose parents were divorced or abusive, and I'd expected my charges to suffer through adjustments to the birth of siblings and moving to new houses. I had been prepared to react with support and understanding to all these childhood traumas, yet not once in any of my classes had the possibility ever been mentioned that the parent of one of my students might die. Nor did I have any idea where to go for guidance in handling the little girl's loss.

Later, when I pulled myself together, I talked to her alone. She told me that her father had fallen off the roof of their house. Her mother had called the ambulance. They took her father to the hospital, but they couldn't make him better. He died. Fumbling my way through our conversation, I hugged her and told her that I was sorry. I offered to talk to her any time she missed her father and wanted to tell me about it, but the school year was over and she went on to another teacher.

I was amazed that a child could have been in my class for five months before I learned that her father had died. Suddenly I was aware that I'd missed opportunities during the year when she might have tried to tell me of her loss. Tossing out the seedlings we were growing, after they died of dehydration over Easter vacation, to avoid the children's disappointment had been a mistake. I also regretted having flushed the occasional dead fish down the toilet before a child could find the bloated, floating body. And when the gerbils had eaten their babies, I couldn't possibly tell the children the horrible truth. The babies were just gone.

I taught for two years after that without having to face the death of a student's parent again. Eventually I had my own children. Although I was more open with Marc and Lara when they encountered death in nature like a crushed bird or squished worm or shriveled plant, we didn't have our first pet funeral until after Don died.

Not that the opportunity hadn't presented itself. The summer before Don died, Marc's hamster, Scotchie, died of old age. One morning Don found him rigid in his cage and quickly disposed of him in the trash can. To give the appearance that Scotchie had escaped, we pried one corner of the cage cover up, and after breakfast we told Marc the sad news that his hamster was "missing." After a few minutes of fake searching Don and I concluded for Marc's benefit that Scotchie must have gotten outside through some crack in the wall. Even though we painted the picture of Scotchie happily roaming the cornfields behind the house, Marc felt rejected by his hamster's quick exit. Pointing to the possibility that Scotchie left to seek out other hamsters, we urged Marc to still consider himself Scotchie's favorite human. Marc did miss Scotchie, but he and Don eventually purchased Scotchie II. Meanwhile Don was spared the agony of confronting death with his five-year-old son, an agony made too intense by Don's knowledge that he could be dying. Don simply couldn't face watching his son mourn a pet hamster because he could envision all too easily Marc mourning even more painfully for his dead father.

Marc and Lara, however, had missed a good opportunity to learn about death in a way that was less traumatic than the death of a parent. When a similar opportunity arose a year and a half after Don died, we handled it differently. One morning Lara found her pet goldfish floating at the top of its jar. She had owned it only overnight, having adopted it the day before at her nursery school's annual picnic. The goldfish, subjected to various learning experiments by its new owner, had had a grueling day in the hot outdoors. Lara's teachers had given her a sheet of questions, like "What happens to the goldfish when you stir the

water one way and then suddenly stir the other way?" I wasn't
surprised that the fish died. Lara cried, though. The three of us
put the fish in one of those single-serving cereal boxes and
buried it in the garden next to the scraggly pine tree that Lara
had planted for Arbor Day. We all said a few words about how
we would miss the fish and how sad we were that it died. I
comforted Lara with the thought that her fish would become
part of the ground that nourished her tree and so, in a sense,
was immortal. We wanted to sing a song, but somehow couldn't
come up with one that had the right flavor. Lara finally insisted
on "This Old Man." Better than "The Worms Crawl In," I had
thought. Then Marc found a large, smooth stone to place on the
grave for a marker. We said good-bye and retired to the house
for a snack. All in all, the fish funeral had been satisfying.
However, it had taken the death of my husband and a great deal
of work with grief on my part to become comfortable enough to
share this experience with my children.

Part of the problem adults have when talking to anyone
newly bereaved is the fear of saying the wrong thing. How
many times have we heard someone confess, "I don't know
what to say." We feel obliged to offer some words of wisdom to
comfort the griever when, in reality, there are no such words.
Adults feel that obligation especially toward children because it
is the grown-ups' role to provide comfort and protection. In
addition, adults often talk down to children, underestimating
their ability to understand. All the clichés that adults use to
avoid the word *death* with other adults become half truths and
lies that confuse children.

Don't say to a child, "We lost Grandma." If she is lost,
then why aren't you out looking for her? If she is *lost,* she can
be *found,* and the child may engage in endless searching behavior. Children need to be told that death is permanent.

Saying "He has gone to his eternal rest" or "eternal
sleep" blurs the distinction between death and sleep and may
lead the child to fear sleep and to suffer insomnia. Again, *sleep*
is not permanent. Someone who sleeps will wake up. How can
people be buried in coffins if they are only sleeping?

Saying "The good die young" isn't helpful, either. If that

is true, then the child is either bad or about to die. Both are disturbing thoughts.

"Mommy went away" could make the child feel abandoned and rejected. If Mommy went away voluntarily, then the child may develop tremendous guilt, thinking he or she did something so terrible that Mommy wanted to leave.

When a child tells you of the death of a parent or other family member, there are a few simple things that you can do immediately. Adults, too, appreciate these expressions of sympathy upon the death of a loved one.

First, tell the child "I'm sorry." Adults who express their condolences to other adults as a matter of courtesy often ignore mourning children for fear of adding to their pain. Yet it is being ignored that causes hurt.

During this simple expression of sympathy, establish eye contact with the child. This tells the child that you care and that you are attentive and ready to listen. You may have to kneel to get on the child's level rather than looking down to them.

Next, if you mean it, offer to listen to the child now or at any time in the future. It's better not to say, "I know just how you feel," because you don't. One of the most effective phrases to lead into a conversation is, "It must be hard for you." This shows the griever that the listener is willing to listen to uncomfortable feelings and to accept them as valid. If the griever does not want to talk, accept that, too. Say sincerely, "Any time you need someone to talk to, please tell me. I will listen." Then be silent to prove what you have said. Just being with the griever in silence is sometimes the most effective expression of sympathy.

Finally, try a touch. A pat on the shoulder or hand, a stroke of the arm, or a hug can be more comforting than any words. Children are usually much more receptive to physical affection than adults. Rarely, a child may pull back. It may be the wrong time or the wrong person. Occasionally a child may not like to be touched, although if the child is avoiding physical contact with everyone, professional counseling may be a good idea.

These are really very simple suggestions—say "I'm

sorry," establish eye contact, listen, and touch. They ought to be learned by everyone, just as all children are taught nowadays to stop, drop, and roll should their clothing catch fire.

An empathetic adult who sincerely offers to talk to the child about the death, about the changes in the child's life his loss has wrought, and especially about the child's feelings whenever the child needs a friend can help him or her recognize and master the powerful feelings of grief.

Most people find it awkward to discuss death, not knowing what to say after "I'm sorry." The following questions, for bereaved adults as well as grieving youngsters, might help people feel more prepared to talk to mourning children.

1. What was the name of the person who died?
2. What do you miss about _____?
3. In what ways can you keep your memories of _____ alive?
   (You might discuss planting a tree, writing a poem, writing a book of memories, drawing a picture, or singing songs.)
4. Can you tell me about the death? What happened that day?
5. What adjustments have you made in your life without _____?
6. Can you tell me about your life with _____?
7. What have you noticed has happened since the death?
8. What changes have happened to you?
9. Can you tell me how you are feeling about your loss today?

It is important to use the dead person's name in the conversation whenever possible. People are often reluctant to mention the name of the deceased. That reluctance does not escape the mourner's attention, and many become resentful that no one will mention their loved one's name. When people seem to be trying to forget that the deceased ever existed, they invalidate the mourner's feeling of loss.

Sometimes bereaved children seem to want to talk but

won't answer direct questions, finding them too threatening or anxiety-provoking. It may help these youngsters to draw on their natural talent for fantasy. Try creating an imaginary scenario for the child and let the child respond. Say something like, "A child wakes up in the morning and feels afraid. What do you think he or she is afraid of?" Children may feel freer to express their emotions under the guise of fiction. The conversation may be depersonalized enough to break through children's anxiety about broaching feelings like anger and guilt.

Many adults are reluctant to talk to bereaved children because adults do not know what to do when a child expresses sadness or anger.

One ten-year-old boy whose mother died went to his bed and curled up in a fetal position, refusing to move or communicate with anyone. Several adults attempted to cajole him out of his stupor, to no avail. "Don't cry," they told him. "Everything will be fine." "Cheer up." "Be brave, little man."

Finally, his playmate from next door was allowed to see him. The little boy looked at his friend lying on the bed and then curled up beside him, saying simply, "I miss your mother, too." After a while both boys got out of bed and the bereaved child could begin to heal.

Those falsely comforting statements commonly made by adults deny bereaved children the expression of their true feelings. The only alternative they are left with is to bottle up those feelings inside. Yet a simple statement which says, "I share your grief in some small way," shows your acceptance of a bereaved child just as she or he is, even if that is sad or angry. It is far better to cry with a child than to inhibit the child's crying. Adult tears show acceptance of children's tears.

Rather than trying to suppress the child's anger, adults should encourage children to express it in acceptable ways. A set of large cardboard blocks like those found in nursery schools is useful in venting anger. Allow the child to build a wall and then kick it down, brick by brick, while verbalizing the anger. It is important to encourage (but not insist on) an "I'm angry because . . ." statement with each kick so that the child becomes comfortable expressing anger in words. Eventually the verbal expression will be enough.

Another idea is to let the child build a scream box. Any closed cardboard box with a paper towel tube inserted in a hole will work. Encourage the child to scream through the tube into the box. Most will end up laughing.

If a child is prone to expressing anger by punching schoolmates or siblings, teach him or her to hit one clenched fist into the other hand instead of lashing out at others. Boys especially take to this because their macho film idols do the same thing.

All of these outlets for anger will probably need to be modeled by the helping adult before the child will try such "silly" actions.

More suggestions for using newspaper, clay, foam bats, punching bags, and hammers and nails to vent anger can be found in Claudia Jewett's book, *Helping Children Cope with Separation and Loss.*

In addition to talking to bereaved children and supporting them when they express their feelings, adults can also help by allowing and encouraging therapeutic play. Although it was not always pleasant to watch my children act out death scenes, some R-rated for violence, I gave both Marc and Lara the freedom to use play for therapy whenever they needed to, which was often. Many times I left them alone so that my presence would not inhibit their self-expression. Occasionally I eavesdropped or even participated.

Sometimes they enjoyed the simplicity of the stereo-typical acting out of death. Marc would stretch out on the coffee table or floor completely immobile and tell his sister, "Let's play dead, La."

They were much more likely, however, to talk through their toy figures or dolls when grappling with their feelings about their father's death. How often I heard Lara, especially, talking for her playthings when she was really speaking for herself. Particularly during the fall after her father's death, when she was struggling so hard to understand her loss, I would hear her alter her voice and have her doll say, "My daddy died." The toys did not even have to be human-like to be enlisted in the children's play. Familiar with talking animals from their hours of cartoon-watching and from children's books, Marc and Lara frequently made stuffed animals or other toy creatures their mouthpieces.

I overheard my two budding vegetarians playing with their farm-animal sets one day. Both children had selected tiny pigs and were talking in appropriately squeaky voices.

"Your daddy is dead," Marc's pig sadly informed Lara's pig. "He's being made into bacon."

"I don't want my daddy to be dead," Lara's pig squealed.

Marc's favorite medium for therapeutic play was his huge collection of Star Wars figures. Lara used them, too, especially the female Leias, but her favorite doll, Honey, seemed to be better able to help her find the courage to express her sadness. As she stuck Honey in my face one day a few months after Don's death, she announced through the doll in a high-pitched voice, "My daddy died!" Then she dropped the doll and reverted to her own voice. "I wish Daddy were real," she said with a sigh. Sometimes, as a three-year-old struggling to understand death, she had difficulty fathoming the difference between inanimate dolls and her dead father.

In the beginning of their mourning both Marc and Lara used therapeutic play to undo their father's death. Once, while Marc and I were playing with his Star Wars figures for the second day in a row, he instructed me: "Make Princess Leia cry because Luke's dead."

"Boo hoo!" I overdramatized.

"Make her listen to see if his heart is beating. She can't hear it. Make her cry," Marc directed.

"Boo hoo, I miss him," I sobbed until Marc had had enough.

"Make her fix him. He's all better," Marc magically pronounced. But Luke died again countless times from laser blasts, spaceship crashes, or body-ripping alien monsters.

Lara, too, used play to undo magically what had been done to her father. Selecting an instrument from her Fisher-Price doctor kit, she would bend over her favorite doll. "She has a lump in her tube that shouldn't be there," she'd diagnose. "Let's operate to fix her broken tube." Surgery was short. "There, she's all better."

At these times I often doubted that their play was actually therapeutic. I had to remind myself that however unrealistic it seemed to me, their play was one good way for them to work through the phases of denial, anger, bargaining, and depression. It would do no good for me to try to direct them to play more realistically, requiring the dead to stay dead. That acceptance would have to come from them when they were ready. I didn't want to disturb their play and inhibit their emotional expression. I tried, therefore, to join in the spirit of the therapeutic play and accept their antics as an expression of where they were in grief. It was enough to reinforce the truth when answering their direct questions about their father's death and death in general.

Their sometimes ingenious play not only provided an outlet for them to express their feelings but also told me when they had troubling concerns. One day before Lara had given up her high chair, she sat at lunch grasping a fork in one hand and a spoon in the other. The spoon spoke first: "Don't worry, dear. Mommy's just going to the office. I'll be right back."

The fork asked in a high-pitched voice, "You won't die, Mommy?"

"No," the spoon reassured the fork.

This interchange informed me that fear of my death was distressing Lara. I was then able to reassure Lara directly by bringing up the subject.

Overhearing my children's play could also give me clues to where they were in their developmental concept of death. One day Lara examined her paper Snoopy doll in his stretched-out position for sleeping on the doghouse roof. "Snoopy is dead and he's never waking up," she confided to me morosely.

Glad to see that Lara was expressing the concept of permanence, I nonetheless followed her mood. "Oh, that's sad," I agreed.

Marc and Lara felt close enough to each other to indulge in therapeutic play together, despite their age difference of three years. Sometimes they invited me to join in, which let me know more about which phase of grief they were working through and how their concept of death was developing. Shared therapeutic play also kept lines of communication open and allowed us to give each other sympathy and support in yet another way.

Therapeutic play is an unstructured way of helping a bereaved child, and it has to come from within that child. About the only thing an adult can do is to provide the materials and the time without distractions like television.

There are more structured ways of helping a bereaved child, some of which may appeal to older children more than therapeutic play. Younger children, too, can benefit from them.

Just as the written word is a useful tool of self-expression and catharsis for the bereaved parent, so it is for the mourning child. Older children might be encouraged to keep a journal in prose or poetry so that they can pour out on paper their feelings of grief. Let them know that you and other adults will respect their privacy and will not read anything in the journal unless invited to do so. You can, however, ask from time to time if there is anything written in the journal that the child might like to share and talk about. Sometimes it is less threatening for children to read aloud what they feel than to try to find the words spontaneously. Even young children can "write" a journal with an adult who is willing to take dictation for them. Helping a young child with diary entries may strengthen communication between both participants.

An adult may also want to help the child prepare a life-book about the person who died. Such a collected history may contain pictures of that person from childhood on, including important events like birth, graduation, wedding, and birthdays. If you don't have photographs, the child can draw his or her own pictures. Children who are reluctant to draw may enjoy cutting out photos of clothing from magazines to paste beneath hand-drawn faces. Any other documents—from birth announcements to obituaries—add to the richness of the history. You may want to label the pages or briefly explain them in writing.

To accompany the life-book, or as a project in itself, you can work with the bereaved child to make a time line incorporating both the important events in the person's life and in world history, giving the children a sense that their loved one had a significant place in this world. Both life-books and time lines help a child realize that there were many things the dead parent did beyond what the child experienced personally. Children thus gain a sense of completeness about the life of their parent—a sense of the naturalness of the cycle of birth and death. Most important though, they preserve their memories of their loved ones.

Many of the suggestions for how the surviving parent can help children through mourning can be used by family friends and relatives as well. Friends and relatives can help the surviving parent prepare photo albums of the child and parent together, especially if the friend or relative has some pictures the family doesn't. They can also help find and frame photographs of the dead parent. I located one photograph of Don through a private photographer who had taken publicity photos for Don's employer. I'd never seen the picture until it was printed in the company paper with Don's obituary. Others can also help by locating any tape recordings that may exist of the loved one and by having copies made for the family. The deceased may have made or purchased gifts that a friend or relative is willing to give the child, too. Simply saying, "Your father [or mother] made [or bought] this for me. I thought you might like to have it." Even if the surviving parent has already given the child some of the dead parent's possessions and clothing for comfort, the child will usually still treasure a friend's or relative's sacrifice. Write a sympathy letter to the child—not a purchased card, but a letter that tells the child a story or fact about the dead parent that the family didn't already know. Participate in Remember Daddy [or Mommy] Time. A friend or relative may remember something that both surviving parent and child have forgotten.

There are countless ways for friends, relatives, and other adults to help the grieving child. But perhaps no other adult, aside from the surviving parent, has as much influence over the mourning child as does the teacher. By virtue of the frequency of their interaction with children, teachers are among the most significant adults in a child's life. Although teachers can help in any of the ways already mentioned, being the teacher of a bereaved child involves special opportunities and responsibilities.

One of the first things a teacher must do is to tell the child's classmates of the death of their fellow student's parent or relative. Informing the class is difficult, and teachers are often reluctant to tackle it. The conscientious teacher should call the parents of each very young child and ask them to talk to their own child about their little friend's loss. If the children are older than six or seven, they can be informed directly by the teacher. Ideally, the students may already have had classroom experiences with death—school pets or plants—which could help them understand. Students and teacher could also discuss books they have read about death, and even act out with puppets some of their feelings about the death of a person they have known.

Children are also good givers of sympathy. A bereaved child who receives sympathy cards from classmates may have less fear of going back to school and facing them. Even adults feel better when they know that their friends know and care.

Teachers can also help the bereaved student by keeping the surviving parent informed of the child's actions, thoughts, and feelings, both bad and good, that relate to the loss. Working together, teacher and surviving parent can help the child by exchanging information and observations that the other may not be aware of. Knowing that the teacher will help tend to the bereaved child's problems allows the surviving parent to worry a bit less.

Teachers should also be prepared to give the bereaved student extra time and attention. There may be tears, lost homework, failed tests, and forgotten lunches. There may be fights between formerly fast friends or withdrawal into isolation. Some teachers may not recognize that these changes are a result of grief, while others, though, recognizing the connection, may be uncomfortable with these strong manifestations of grief. Punishing the bereaved child for behavior changes will only exacerbate the problem. All of the previous suggestions for channeling anger and other emotions into more acceptable outlets for expression can be used in the classroom. Communication between teacher and bereaved child is essential, and teachers should not hesitate to use whatever school counseling resources are available to maximize that communication. Perhaps most importantly, teachers must understand that working through the grieving process takes a long time and that bereaved children may not return to their normal behavior until after they have gone on to another teacher. Even then there may be permanent changes.

Another way teachers can help children mourn is to recognize that the definition of such traditions as Mother's Day and Father's Day should be broadened. After the experience with my first little bereaved pupil and my own son's anxiety about what do do with his handmade Father's Day gift, I know how difficult these holidays are for bereaved children. Children's feelings of exclusion can be relieved by explaining that Father's Day is a day to say thank you to *all* the men who help children throughout the year: grandfathers, uncles, cousins, older brothers, next-door neighbors, and even teachers. Mother's Day should be given the same freedom of interpretation, too. Instead of having each child make only one card or gift, teachers could give students the opportunity to make as many as they have people they want to thank. Children, especially bereaved children, need to share their love openly with all those who care for them.

Marc and Lara's therapeutic play at home convinced me that providing an opportunity for such play in classrooms can keep teachers more informed about their student's progress through the phases of grief. All pupils' understanding of death can be discerned by observing their play. Therapeutic play also offers teachers and classmates the chance to express their sympathy for the bereaved child.

One of the most important ways teachers, friends, and relatives can help children is through books and reading. Both of my children enjoyed school and delighted in learning, especially through their favorite friends, books. If their bookbags flopped empty on their backs as they ran to catch the school bus each morning, they weighed their owners down on the short march home in the afternoon. Caring teachers can use children's natural association of books with school to provide help for both the bereaved child and other students through bibliotherapy.

Joanne E. Bernstein, in her excellent *Books to Help Children Cope with Separation and Loss,* explains bibliotherapy as reading that results in self-examination and gained insights. Teachers needn't wait for a classroom crisis to use bibliotherapy. Although it helps students with problems find solutions for coping, it also allows them to develop solutions to future problems. Preparing for life's challenges in calmer, less emotional times can benefit all children when they eventually face the turmoil of loss.

In the classroom, bibliotherapy can be both spontaneous or directed. To encourage the former, every classroom and school library should contain a selection of books, bulletin boards displaying book jackets, and annotated reading lists of books for children coping with death. Book reports by students or teachers and reading books aloud during library time are other ways of arousing interest. Children can then choose the book that meets their needs, whether they're generally interested in learning about death or specifically seeking help for bereavement. Mourning children, in fact, may not immediately choose to read a book on death but may wait until they are ready to face their grief.

Directed bibliotherapy involving the whole class is excellent for preparing children to face loss, but should be used with care immediately after a student's parent dies. Grieving children should never be singled out and made to feel that their loss is a problem which makes them different from their classmates. Teachers should use their judgment to decide when the whole class or reading group should read and discuss a book on death—perhaps when the bereaved child is absent for the funeral, or after enough time has passed so that the child will not feel that the choice is solely for his or her benefit. Having students read the story aloud and retell it, answering questions about its facts, talking about the characters' actions and feelings, and giving personal opinions are techniques of directed bibliotherapy familiar to all reading teachers. Parents, relatives and family friends can use these techniques when they read with their mourning children.

Be prepared for the child's own experience of loss to pop out, something which happens not only during bibliotherapy but spontaneously when the child feels the need and has the freedom to confide in an empathetic relative, friend, teacher, or other adult. Above all, you should always remember that perhaps the greatest comfort you or any other adult can give to a grieving child is to listen.

A NEW LIFE

We moved to Michigan late in August, nineteen months after Don died, and I felt we were ready to leave our old life behind. The small house we were building was only a quarter of a mile down a wooded path from the children's grandparents. Their lakefront homestead also included the cottage where our family had spent many a lazy summer vacation when Don was alive. We were fortunate, moving to a familiar place with cherished memories and two wonderful people to give us love and support.

For the first three months we lived with my parents while our house was being built. Because we had spent the entire summer in the same place the year before, Marc already had friends nearby. Benji and Michael, the sons of an old high school chum of mine, Dave, and his wife, Lynn, lived across the lake. We traded baby-sitting, but I think Marc and Lara got the better deal. When I told them Dave would watch them one afternoon, Marc said, "He's not my father, but he's pretty close. Great!" Lara said, "He makes cookies with me. Oh, boy!" Both Marc and Lara enjoyed playing with Michael and Benji, but none of the children were in the same grade in school. Next door to our new house were three other boys, Ben, Erik, and their baby brother, Joe. Ben was in Marc's grade at school.

Even though Marc had one friend in his class at his new school in the fall, he was concerned about fitting in with the rest of his second-grade classmates. As soon as school started in September, the children began carefully planning for the annual parent open house. When Marc delivered his hand-printed invitation to me, he remarked, "My dad can't come, but a lot of other dads won't be able to come either. They'll be at work."

I hated to dash his hopes that no one would notice he didn't have a father, but I thought he should be prepared. "Most dads will probably come, Marc," I corrected. "The meeting is at night." Marc sadly shuffled outside to play. The open house turned out to be nothing to worry about. Other fathers were absent, either working the night shift or home watching a ball game on TV.

Both of my children had been fortunate to have warm and supportive teachers each year since the death of their father, and in Michigan that pattern continued. To avoid a shock like I experienced in my first year of teaching, I informed each new teacher that my children's father had died. It was helpful to Marc that his second-grade class was in the hands of a master teacher. She was genuinely fond of him, and he loved school. He did not have any problems in school as a result of his father's death or from the necessary adjustment that followed. In fact, he excelled in his studies, eventually enrolling in a program for students with high academic potential.

Marc did not just breeze through the adjustment to our move to Michigan, however. At first he was not altogether happy about being uprooted. One day while the two of us walked back from the Betsie River Bridge near where the house was being built, he complained to me, "Everything is different in Michigan, even my friends."

"You have as much fun with your friends here as you did in New Jersey, don't you?" I asked.

"Yes," he admitted. "But they do different things here. Ben doesn't play the same way that Chad and I used to play. It's just different."

Marc's brief period as an outsider didn't seem to harm

him much. He, Ben, and Erik eventually became fast friends, developing the same feelings of brotherhood, of belonging as he'd had in his old neighborhood. Marc had always been an empathetic child, but during his adjustment he seemed to develop an even broader perspective on his friends. More and more he reminded me of his father.

One of his first invitations out was given by a boy who came from a family of eight. Marc rode the bus home with his friend, and I picked him up later in the evening. When I knocked on the door and was admitted to a sparsely furnished, tattered living room, I wondered how they had been able to afford to feed Marc. In the car, I asked him if he had enjoyed his afternoon. He said, "Yes," and after a rundown on his activities with his friend he was quiet for a moment.

Finally he said, "I think they're poor, Mom." I thought so, too, but Marc's simple statement made me stop looking down my nose long enough to look straight ahead. It is sometimes easier to feel empathy for an outsider when you are an outsider, too.

When Marc started second grade, Lara was old enough for kindergarten. I was prepared for a renewal of separation anxiety, since we had just moved, and I fully expected the same nursery school tears and screaming as the yellow bus rolled up on the first day of public school. When the bus doors folded open, Lara said, "'Bye, Mom," and gave me a quick kiss. She hopped up the stairs of the bus, and after turning to wave briefly, she plopped down into a seat next to another little wide-eyed girl. As the bus pulled away from me, I was the one who cried.

Although Lara adjusted well to kindergarten socially, she lagged behind most of her classmates academically. She was not yet five when I enrolled her in school, but she had passed the screening test with flying colors. I reasoned that if I held her back in nursery school she would end up having to adjust to two new schools instead of one. I started her in kindergarten with the thought that she could repeat it if necessary and still be in the same familiar environment with the same teacher. That is almost what happened, except that in the spring she had a learning spurt and seemed to catch on to her letter sounds. Her teacher said that she couldn't recommend that Lara be held back.

Unfortunately for Lara, the same pattern would repeat itself until I had her tested for learning disabilities. We discovered that she was farsighted and needed glasses, and had a muscle problem that caused eye underconvergence. The effort she had to make just to focus her eyes on a letter or word could distract from her concentration on learning to read. That problem would be one she would have to live with the rest of her life, though it could be helped by a program of eye exercises.

She also showed signs of a developmental lag of about six months in coordination. When she was a toddler, Don's father used to joke that she would be a surgeon someday, because she was so good with her eye-hand coordination. I often wondered if the loss of her father retarded that development. Some research suggests that when a child's parent dies during a crucial time in the development of a certain skill, the child may miss that skill development and never catch up. The child may focus in on the emotional stress instead of reaching outward to explore the world.

When Lara started kindergarten, I was more concerned about her continued struggle to understand and accept her father's death than I was with how fast she would learn to read or how coordinated she was compared to other five-year-olds. Just as Marc was self-conscious about being different from the other children in his new environment, Lara, too, began to get a glimmer that she was different from the norm.

"Nana cried when Daddy died," she remembered one day as we walked quietly to the school bus stop. "She was sad because he was her son. When I die my mommy and daddy will cry. No . . . I don't have a daddy," she suddenly realized how she was different. "Just my mommy. Why did Daddy have to die?" she asked me earnestly.

"I don't know," I answered honestly. "We just weren't very lucky, I guess."

"Yes, but I wish Daddy didn't die," she insisted.

"So do I."

Still puzzled, still desperately seeking a reason for the

inexplicable, and still believing in her own control over her world, she asked me one more time, "Why did Daddy have to die?"

One consolation was that Lara's memories of him continued to crop up from time to time, triggered by specific activities. I had worried that moving from the house we shared with her father would make it even more difficult for her to remember him. I worried less after she proved my concern groundless. One warm fall day she was playing in a sandpile at the base of the deck her grandfather was building. Shoveling damp sand over her feet, she asked, "Do you remember what Daddy let us do to him?"

"No. What?" I wondered.

"You know," she answered impatiently. "How we used to cover his feet up with sand." She stared at her own hidden toes.

"Yes, now I remember." I nodded. I really had forgotten the details of all those trips to the beach in Connecticut when Don was having radiation therapy.

A month later her grandfather was standing in the same spot, raking gravel to cover the sandpile. Lara watched, then said, "Daddy used to rake the grass." The five-year-old child had dredged up memories stored by her two-year-old baby-self for safekeeping.

Lara's cognitive development had progressed to the point where, armed with a much better ability with language, she was asking the same kinds of unpleasant questions that Marc had asked immediately after Don died. I had to screw up my courage to guide my second child through the concrete facts of Don's death. The first time with Marc had been unpleasant enough, and reliving Don's death with Lara disturbed my own equilibrium.

As Lara and I rode together in the car one day, she asked, "Did they take Daddy's skin off when he died?"

I guessed that she was wondering how a body turned into a skeleton. "No. What made you think of that?" I asked.

"I had a dream about it last night," she calmly admitted to my horror. "They just buried him in a box?"

"Yes, the box is called a *coffin*. He was buried just the way he was. He was buried with his clothes on, too." I was trying to paint her a more pleasant picture of her father's body.

"It's not nice to talk about Daddy, is it?" she whispered guiltily. Just the night before I had heard her say to her brother, "I miss Daddy."

He'd chastised her, saying vehemently, "Don't talk about it."

At times the stress of adjusting to a new environment seemed to prompt Marc to avoid the strain of longing. I tried to explain his feelings to Lara. "It's hard, sometimes, to talk about Daddy dying, but it's easier to talk about how much he loved us."

By late October most of the children's adjustment anxiety was replaced by anticipation of their favorite holiday, Halloween. I borrowed my mother's sewing machine to make Marc a Viking costume out of fake fur. Lara, a ballerina in her pink tutu, wore a sweatsuit underneath to keep her warm for trick-or-treating. I had to drive them around because the houses of the few people we knew were too far apart for walking. The children didn't get as much loot as they used to when we lived in a subdivision, but they were happy. As a special treat, they were allowed to stay out late for the Halloween concert at the Interlochen Arts Academy. It was definitely the highlight of the evening, with *Danse Macabre*, conducted by a vampire amidst eerie dry-ice smoke.

As we rode home after the concert, Marc and Lara sat chatting in the back seat of the car.

"That was the best Halloween ever!" Lara bubbled.

I grinned from the front seat until I heard Marc's retort. "Nah! The best was with Daddy!"

For the children's birthdays, which soon followed, Marc's eighth and Lara's fifth, they had pizza parties with their new friends in their grandparents' basement. We moved into our new house at Thanksgiving. I hung the same old curtains and furnished the living room with the same old sofas. The kitchen cupboards held the same dishes, and the same pictures hung on our walls, including our family portrait in the same place over the dry sink. At night, we snuggled to sleep in the same warm beds. Thanksgiving and Christmas were both spent quietly with my parents, continuing the tradition we'd begun the year before.

We settled down into a comfortable routine of home and school. About the only outside interest I had was attending the meetings and social events of the American Association of University Women. After so many months of feeling as if my social skills had regressed to the level of a fourteen-year-old, I found it a low-key way to get back into socializing: in a women's club it didn't matter that I didn't have a spouse, and I never felt left out for being single.

Even if I'd never broadened my social circle, it would have been impossible to avoid all remembrances of my single status, and neither could the children escape reminders that they were without a father. Stuck inside on a snowy day, Marc was watching reruns when a Mormon commercial honoring fatherhood came on the TV screen. A song burst out, "When she skinned her knee riding her bike, Dad, who kissed the hurt? When he needed help figuring those sums, Dad, who lent a hand? When she didn't feel much like going to school, Dad, who drove her there? Who is always there when they need you, Dad? You are!"

"I hate that!" Marc spat. "I feel like everyone in the world has a daddy but me."

I hugged him. "I know it seems that way sometimes, but there are lots of children who don't have daddies. That doesn't help much when it's you, does it?"

No, it doesn't.

One morning Marc crawled in bed with me earlier than usual. Instead of cuddling he was busily finishing his homework for school. I was still half asleep.

"Would 'Marc and Lara's dog is good' be with an *s apostrophe?* I have to write about this picture," he said as he shoved his workbook in front of my bleary eyes.

"How about 'The children's dog is good'?" I suggested with a yawn.

"I don't know how to spell *children,*" Marc whined, sounding upset.

"C-h-i-l-d-r-e-n," I spelled, rolling over to look at the book again. "But *children's* is with an *apostrophe s.*"

"But I need an *s apostrophe,*" Marc insisted.

I squinted without my glasses. "That's not a girl and a boy in the picture. They are both girls. 'The girls' dog' would be *s apostrophe.*" I added, "I wish you'd use pencil instead of ink."

"I can't," Marc complained. "None of my pencils have points!"

"Well, if you'll put them in the kitchen, I'll sharpen them," I snapped. "Now you'll have to write the right sentence underneath."

Marc wrote the sentence, examined his less-than-per-fect-looking paper, and began to cry.

I was sorry I'd been short-tempered with him. "What's the matter, Marc? Why are you so upset? It's okay."

"I miss Daddy," he sniffed. Daddy would have helped him do it right the first time.

I missed him, too, I told Marc, and we cried together. Even in our new life, we still keenly felt the absence of our husband and father.

And even though I was making new friends, there were times I felt desperately lonely, and ashamed for feeling that way. I had two beautiful children to keep me company and my friends and parents were unfailingly helpful, including us in their social activities. But it just wasn't the same. Those rela-tionships were not what I was lonely for. I was lonely for a man, not just any man, but a man who knew me better and loved me more than anyone in the world, as Don had.

Although I was beginning to long for some male com-panionship, I was also apprehensive about entering the dating scene after so many years of marriage. All the rules had changed, and I wasn't sure that I liked the new ones. I also worried about the effect dating would have on the children, even though outwardly they seemed to accept and even encour-age the idea of remarriage.

The first thing that Marc had said to me the night I'd told him his father had just died was, "Don't worry, Mommy. You can marry someone else." During the years that followed Don's death, Marc's continued pondering of a new father was not just an attempt to deny his loss by filling the void. To him, security was linked with having a new father. As the five-year-old son of a friend said when she announced she was getting remarried two years after her husband died, "Well, Mom, if you die, at least I'll still have a parent."

Marc had shown signs of missing the security of having a father as soon as Don died. Shortly after our memorable trip to the Franklin Institute in Philadelphia with Ken and Sharon's family, Sharon and I had planned another outing. Marc had been excited when I told him to get ready.

"Is Ken going to the movies with us?" he'd asked eagerly.

"No, he has a meeting," I'd answered with regret. "Sharon and the kids are coming."

Marc had been disappointed. "He reminds me of Daddy. He's nice like Daddy. Couldn't you marry him?"

"He's already married to Sharon," I'd said, chuckling.

"He's my second daddy," Marc had cheerfully announced.

When the subject of remarriage had cropped up again over Saturday morning pancakes, Marc had asked, "When you are married to someone and they die, can you marry someone else?" And then: "Mom, will you marry someone else?"

He hadn't been happy when I'd told him that I wasn't ready to marry anyone else yet because I still loved his father too much. "I'm ready *now*," Marc had said, as if that settled that matter. "But it will be hard to find someone who isn't already married. We'll have to look all over the world!"

I'd laughed to myself, imagining the search through arid deserts and breezy tropics. "You don't go looking for someone," I'd told him. "You just go on living, and if you meet someone you fall in love with, you marry him."

There were times when I began to wonder if Marc's technique for finding companionship might not be more productive. My way didn't bring me my first date until nearly two years after Don died. I did have a lot of near misses, though. There was the blue-eyed plumber who bent over my bathtub for an hour while I perched on the toilet seat drinking coffee and pretending to be fascinated with his graphic description of breeding hunting dogs. Unfortunately, his partner returned to finish the job. And there was the handsome fellow student I managed to sit next to every single week in one of my education courses, until he confided in me that he was a monk on temporary leave from his monastery.

The most promising brush was with a former pro-basketball player who happened to be sitting alone on a train to New York City. This was when I was taking Marc and Lara to see the circus in Madison Square Garden before we moved. No, he didn't mind if we sat down in the other three seats. After a few kind words and pats to the little ones, he said, "Do you get to New York often?" He missed my witty reply, "Not as often as I'd like to," because my son, the one who was in a hurry to marry me off, "accidentally" jabbed him in the thigh with a pencil.

So when a friend moaned, "Something must be wrong with me—it's been fifteen months since my husband died and no one has asked me for a date," I could retort, "There's nothing wrong with either of us. Give yourself seven more months."

Another friend, a pretty, blonde widow, had no trouble finding dates, but her dating was sometimes hard on both her and her children. Her daughter complained, "I wish Daddy were still alive. First you're going with someone, and then you're not!"

My male widowed friends didn't seem to be any happier, even though they started dating much sooner after their wives' deaths. One man told me, "I've gone out with a few women, but they just aren't Norma." Another dated one woman steadily for a while, but the relationship ended. "It was physically satisfying," he admitted, "but she just wasn't Joanne." Both men have since remarried. Unlike many widowers, who remarry much sooner on the average than widows, both men had waited more than eighteen months after their wives' deaths before remarrying. More than half the widowers who remarry earlier than that end up divorced. Yet the average amount of time after the death of a spouse until remarriage is only two years for men, but seven years for women.

Just as attempts to replace a spouse may be doomed to failure, so may attempts to replace a parent. Although the relationship between stepparent and child can enrich the lives of both, it seldom equals the lost relationship immediately in quality. My friends Carol and Richard married fifteen years ago when his youngest child was eight years old. Her biggest problem in adjusting to the marriage was her expectation that mutual love would be quick and automatic within her new stepfamily. "You know, Linda," she told me, "when you do remarry, it may take a couple of years for your husband to really love your kids."

"Hey, her kids are lovable," another friend protested.

"I know," she said, smiling.

Living up to children's expectations must be equally as hard on a stepparent as trying to live up to his or her own. When she'd first expressed her opinion, three-year-old Lara had ordered me to find "a new Daddy just like my old one." Her first step in accepting a possible new father was, naturally, to want one similar enough to Don to give her a familiar feeling of security.

Months later Lara was able to accept that her relationship with Don could not be duplicated and to distinguish between her feelings for Don and a possible new father.

"We still love our daddy," she stated. "We'll still love him, even when we have a different daddy."

"Yes, you can love more than one daddy," I assured her.

The children's willingness to accept a new father in their lives was a supreme compliment to their father. The positive feelings Don left with his children about the father-child relationship will, I believe, carry over to their relationships with their own children someday.

When I did start dating, it was not in a way that I had expected. I'd imagined that I would meet some nearby single man, perhaps on one of my forays to the supermarket or library or somewhere ordinary, and he would miraculously ask me for a date. The reality happened more the way Marc had envisioned over pancakes. Just days after I moved us into our new house, I left the children with my parents and took a ten-day trip to Hawaii. It was the reward I had promised myself for making it that far. It was also ten days of much-needed rest and relief from responsibility. To my surprise I also met two men on the trip with whom I kept in contact briefly after my return home. Because these were long-distance relationships, the children never got to know either of the men, which was perhaps for the best. It did, however, give the kids an awareness that their mother might have a social life apart from them.

Soon after that, I dated other men closer by, but sporadically. In fact there were months when I was "between dates." At first the children were sure I was going to marry each man who walked through the front door. Eventually, after protestations that we were just friends, and after a couple of relationships that ended, they accepted that, although we might all get close to someone for a time, it didn't mean I would marry him. They sometimes missed someone they had gotten to know, but to my relief it wasn't the same way they missed their father. I was careful about whom I let get close to us, and I dated very little. The children were not subjected to a constant stream of men passing through the house—and indeed, I couldn't have found a constant stream if I'd wanted to: single men my age were not that easy to meet.

When I wasn't dating (and occasionally when I was), I wallowed in my loneliness for a few hours at a time, sometimes for days or weeks. By the second anniversary of Don's death I had regained enough energy to counteract my bouts of loneliness with worthwhile activities. Yet there were still times, sometimes months on end, when I suffered the awful ache of endless loneliness, when I longed for something more.

In February I was visiting a friend who regularly attended church. When I asked him why, he answered simply, "For spiritual support." My first thought was that I could use some of that. When I accompanied him to church the following Sunday morning, it was the first time in seventeen years that I had set foot in a religious sanctuary for anything other than a wedding, organ recital, or historical tour.

I'd been thinking about religious education for my children for a few months, and after taking that first step, the next step—finding a home church for our family—came easily. One

Sunday I visited the local church of the denomination in which I had been raised. I was so warmly welcomed that by the next Sunday the children were enrolled in Sunday school and the Sunday after that I was wearing a choir robe. I was amazed not only at how comfortable I felt but also at how suddenly my anger with God had dissipated. I was also pleasantly surprised that the children accepted so readily a new religious approach after their early years of Jewish upbringing. Perhaps they understood my attitude that their Christian education would be an addition to rather than a negation of their Jewish heritage. We still continued to celebrate both Christian and Jewish holidays; I wanted the children to maintain a bond with their father through knowledge of his culture.

After Lara had attended Sunday school for a few weeks, she wondered out loud over her bologna sandwich one day, "why" we used to go to Hebrew school and now we go to church.

I answered as simply as I could. "When I was a little girl, I went to church. Then when I married Daddy, we went to a synagogue. Now we don't have Daddy here anymore. I thought for a long time and decided that it was important for me to go to church."

"Do you know why it's important to me?" she asked, ready to share her secret.

"No. Why?"

"Because we learn about Jesus, and Daddy is with other people in heaven," she stated confidently. She had progressed from wanting his spirit for herself to wanting his spirit to be happy.

"Does that make you feel good to know that Daddy isn't alone?" I asked.

"Yes. He's with his ancestors." I pictured his grave among the stones carved with the Star of David in the same cemetery with his grandparents. He would have wanted to be with his ancestors. Lara, though, wondered if there mightn't be a minor disadvantage to the company her father now kept. "Is he with Aunt Margaret?" she asked with barely disguised pity.

Aunt Margaret had been immortalized in my family for being exceedingly fussy. When Lara refused to eat her chicken because the white meat had a tiny brown speck, or when she wouldn't touch her bread because the corner had brushed through the catsup on her hamburger, we called her "Aunt Margaret." No wonder she wasn't pleased that Daddy might have to endure Aunt Margaret's company forever.

I laughed. "Don't worry, Lara," I advised. "Aunt Margaret is my ancestor, not Daddy's." Would I be the one so eternally blessed?

Lara, especially, began to find more comfort in spiritual practices. After a few months of Sunday school attendance she asked me, "When can we pray for Daddy?"

"Any time you want. You can pray for Daddy right now if you want to," I suggested.

"I want to pray tonight. Don't forget."

I didn't, and neither did she. We prayed that night and later, whenever she wanted to ask God to bless Daddy and take good care of him.

I don't know how much Lara's initial attraction to religion was due to the fact that religious ideas about heaven and the afterlife fit neatly into her understanding of the concept of death. Although she had made great progress, at times she still showed magical thinking and a disregard for the permanence of death. To many believers, God is the ultimate magician, all-seeing, all-knowing, all-powerful. Whether God can or does reverse death is a theological question that adults debate. While observing my children grow up, I was frequently amazed by how many theological questions are rooted in our childhood development of conceptual thinking.

I wasn't surprised at Easter when Lara indulged in a little religious magical thinking. Before Easter Sunday morning service our church released hundreds of helium-filled balloons, carrying messages that the children of the church had written on Palm Sunday. The three of us watched in awe as the balloons spiraled upward around the tall steeple before the wind swept them off toward the bay. I asked Lara what message she had written. Still facing skyward she answered, "If you see my daddy, bring him home." She must have thought that her balloon would get to heaven and an angel or even God might read her message.

Marc's adjustment to church was made easier that summer after a week of vacation Bible school based on the curriculum "Marketplace 29 A.D." This program recreated an ancient tent village to teach children what life was like in Jesus' time. The tribes in those times were Jews, and the kids and I were the only members of our church who had any firsthand knowledge of Judaism. With two years of Jewish nursery school under his belt, Marc, especially, was able to display his expertise. For a week we taught the others about Jewish customs and holidays and led prayers and blessings in Hebrew. Marc and Lara were in their glory, having their two religious backgrounds blended so naturally and beautifully. I know the experience gave both of them a more complete sense of belonging to their new church. It was especially significant for Marc, whose identification with his father's heritage was stronger than his sister's. As for me, I will always cherish the moment during our final worship when I stood in the middle of our sanctuary wrapped in Don's prayer shawl and said the Hebrew blessings over the Sabbath candles while more than a hundred small faces gazed at me in awe.

Eventually, I would be elected an elder and called to be our church's Stephen Ministry leader. The Stephen Series is an interdenominational system that trains lay members of a church to be caregivers to those in need. When I was asked to lead it, I felt blessed with joy and real excitement at being given the opportunity and the challenge to use my talents and my experience to help other suffering people.

As Marc, Lara, and I formed our relationship with the church, our spiritual concept of death finally evolved into one we could hold in common. We were comforted by sharing a belief that Don was with God in heaven. Although the way Marc and Lara came to understand that concept might have been somewhat unorthodox, they seemed to grasp intuitively the beliefs that adults write books arguing over. Because they believed God is everywhere, they found no incongruity in believing that Don's spirit could be both in heaven and with us. He commuted.

Our involvement in a church has not been the only way that we have received mutual support while reaching out to help others. About the same time we joined our church, I decided to form another support group for widowed parents, this time with the help of the local hospice. Four people attended the first meeting. At times it swelled to twenty members but usually averaged about eight per meeting. We met in the evening twice a month to discuss our experiences and to take comfort in the knowledge that others were in the same boat. In fact, we learned that the boat was a yacht rather than a dinghy. When someone said, "I know just how you feel," it was true. We talked about ourselves, about our children, and our personal tragedies, all in confidence.

We also shared our triumphs. One member told us how she mustered the courage to take her two young children camping for the first time since her husband died. She had never hooked up the trailer by herself before. Another told us how she went mushrooming alone for the first time and realized, when it began to get dark, that she'd better not cut home through the woods the way she and her husband always had. If she had gotten lost, her son would not know where to find her. She wisely took the long road. A third member told us about the evening that her teen-aged son insisted on taking her out for a movie and dinner afterward with his own money. As mother and son talked about good old times and changing new ones, he confessed to her that he had been looking for something in her drawer and discovered the diary she had kept after her husband died. He was so touched by her record of pain that he wanted to ask her, "How are you doing now, Ma?" He also wanted to share a special bond with her, that of bereaved parent and child.

After meeting with these sensitive, open people, I always felt that I had received more than I had given. I also gained more courage to go on living, making the decisions for our family and making a few mistakes.

One member of the group, Millie, was worried sick about her fourteen-year-old son, Mike, she told us at her first meeting. His father had been killed in an automobile accident six weeks earlier, and Mike had already channeled his grief into drastic behavior changes. He gave up his former friends for a new group that Millie considered the wrong crowd. His school had already contacted Millie to demand that she do something about his slipping grades and belligerent behavior in class. No, the school did not have a counselor with whom Mike could talk.

"Mike and his dad used to do a lot together. They used to talk," Millie informed us. "Mike not only lost his dad; he also lost his best friend."

The rest of us in the support group could only reassure Millie that her son's behavior was normal for a bereaved child and encourage her to continue to give him love, support, and time to heal.

A few months later when the weather warmed up, our group began meeting once a month for family picnics. Several of us lived on lakes, so those outings included swimming, fishing and other water games in addition to regular kids-against-parents volleyball games. For that first picnic we threw some hot dogs into our coolers and dragged our children to the appointed spot, telling them only that every other child there had also suffered the death of a parent and assuring them that they would have fun. They did. Parents began to notice not only that the kids were more easily persuaded to attend our group family functions—no mean feat with teenagers—but also that the children came to understand why we came together for our biweekly informal meetings.

That summer Mike learned how to water ski. The lone man in our original group and a couple of women boating enthusiasts pulled him around a lake or two until the grin on his face showed clearly. He knew he had mastered something he'd been unable to handle before. That little victory, along with the new friendships of our other "special" kids, and his mother's continued love, support, and patience, helped Mike turn himself around. He became an outgoing, cheerful, considerate high school student.

Our formula for the successful participation of our children in our family meetings was simple. First, we planned activities that children of all ages could enjoy. In addition to at least four picnics a year, we had annual Halloween and Christmas parties. On Halloween *everyone,* including adults, wore costumes. On Christmas, parents brought small gifts for their own children, sneaking them into Santa's bag. We also went sledding, bowling, and attended a local barbecue and fair. Game and movie night became a favorite.

We used local talent to bring life to the party, too. One Halloween, a juggler tossed his way into our kids' hearts for a fifth of his usual fee. At Christmas, our Santa suited up absolutely free. We're sure he was Saint Nick because he enticed every single child, from two to twenty, to sit on his lap and accept a present.

We also didn't attempt to formalize the discussions between children. Most of our children were eager to join in family meetings when we reassured them that we did not expect them to sit around and talk about "heavy" things in imitation of our support group meetings. Informal discussions took place between children of all ages spontaneously. We recommended that, before each family event, new participants or younger children be reminded that every child there had a parent who'd died. We didn't necessarily consider a rap group for bereaved children, especially the older ones, a bad idea. We felt, however, that such a group should be distinct from family activities and led by a professional.

We learned, too, to enlist experienced children to draw new children into the group. With older children, a suggestion to include the new boy or girl was usually enough. With younger children, proximity usually initiated cooperative play. Older children were also good at acting as big brother or big sister, especially when the younger child was not their real sibling.

Once in a while, we found, we needed an ice-breaker, an activity in which everyone participated and received support from others. At summer picnics, our volleyball games loosened up adults and children alike. One of our Halloween parties was a bust until we forced everyone ("Or else!") to join the relay race to "break the balloon with your bottom." As the balloons began to burst, the kids began to cheer each other on to greater depths, and by the end of the game, they had become a group that could direct its own next activity. We parents retired to play Trivial Pursuit.

Finally, and above all, we learned that if we enjoyed ourselves, the kids followed suit. We delighted in the pleasure of each other's company, becoming in effect an extended family that offered a network of support and caring to enhance the healing process and enrich the lives of us all.

The social function of our group expanded to include adults-only dinners out. Finding it difficult if not impossible to dine alone in a restaurant, many widowed people don't. Widowed parents need to take time away from their children to recharge their batteries, but often miss the companionship of their spouse so much that they simply sit at home. Our most heavily attended "meetings" were the monthly dinners out. We made it clear, however, that this was only one function of our group, and not the main one. The primary purpose was to help each other work through our grief and facilitate our children's mourning.

There were occasions when dining out was as much an expression of support as a social function. One dinner took place the day before my birthday, a time when my loneliness was always acute. I thought the company would help, but between the salad and the entrée my cheerful veneer cracked and my lip began to quiver. Donna, sitting directly across from me, said, "Go ahead and cry if it will make you feel better. None of us will mind." I didn't cry, though. Just having my pain acknowledged by someone who understood made me feel better.

We also made it clear that our support group was not a dating service. At least we made it clear to one another. I'm not sure that our children didn't have ulterior motives in shipping us off to group meetings, even though there were many more women than men who attended.

After our first picnic I reminded Lara, "All of the children there had a parent who died."

"Everyone lost a daddy except Dick," she said.

"Yes, Dick's children are the only ones whose mommy died," I agreed.

"Will they get a stepmother?" she asked.

"Maybe, someday."

"Will we get a stepfather?" she asked.

"Maybe, someday," I answered.

"I hope so."

In fact, the following winter Dick married Liz, a widow from the group, creating a blended family with seven children. A few others have also remarried, but none within the support group.

Widowed parents who are at a point in the grieving process where they need mutual support but have no group to join or energy to start one can take the small-step approach. Find one other widowed parent to meet with on a regular basis. Your family doctor, minister or rabbi or priest, your children's school, or your local hospice will probably be able to connect you with other widowed parents. Many churches will let you use a meeting room at no charge. Some local newspapers have free weekly listings of area support groups. That and word of mouth may very well attract enough people for a group. If not, at least you will have reached out to one other person in need.

Some say that a sixth phase should be added to our perception of the grieving process and that is the phase I call outreach, reaching out to help others. If acceptance brings us a measure of serenity and reconciliation with reality, outreach builds self-esteem and gives bereaved people an opportunity for self-expression. As "wounded healers," a term originated by Henri Nouwen, we often have developed a greater capacity for empathizing with others' suffering, and our firsthand knowledge allows us to communicate more effectively with those also grieving. Because we're become more proficient and dedicated caregivers, our outreach does make a difference, both to those we've helped and to our own sense of self-worth. We are models to others; inspirations to those who are struggling to survive.

Many of us have a need to create something positive out of our loss, as the phoenix arose from the ashes. For centuries people have memorialized their dead with pyramids and monuments. Others of us channel our creative urge into outreach; by leading support groups, by volunteering, by lecturing, by educating, by communicating our experience in word, song, music, dance, film, art, or any other medium, thereby enriching the lives of others.

Children, too, can be wounded healers. Often the love and expression of sympathy shown to me by Marc and Lara was all that made my pain bearable. From the time of their loss, their growing insight and empathy for other children has distinguished them from their less-experienced peers. The healing power generated by our support group family outings also testifies to children's ability to reach out to others.

Several months after I started the support group in Michigan, another support group was formed in our area, this one for bereaved children, and Marc and Lara began attending. Under the direction of Barbara McIntyre, an art therapist, toddlers to teens gathered in the expansive basement room of a local medical center for two hours each week to draw, paint, sculpt, rip, and chisel as a means of expressing and sharing grief through art. Children of all ages seemed to find it easier to talk about their pictures than to talk about their feelings.

The goals of the art therapy support group were basic: to help clarify children's feelings about the death or imminent loss; to help them better understand that others share their feelings and experiences; to give them the opportunity to learn new communication and coping skills; and to provide an opportunity for them to clarify their attitudes about future love relationships and marriage, their own and their parent's.

Most of the professional artists and other volunteer staff had also suffered a significant loss in their families, so they, too, were wounded healers. At the first session, Marc enviously watched the male camaraderie around the woodworking area; a group of teenage boys seemed to be having such a good time. Dan Gray was the artist assigned especially to work with the older boys because, as a former semi-pro football player, he could talk sports with them and gradually build rapport until they felt comfortable talking about their feelings. Dan's father had died when he was three years old.

Even though Marc didn't spend much time with the big boys, he still enjoyed art therapy, becoming immediately engrossed in whatever project the staff tempted him with. Lara quickly became attached to Ed, a Native American artist who was so gentle with the little children. I was pleased because Lara had always gravitated to women rather than men. Both Marc and Lara asked to come back after the first session. It was another important opportunity for them to be with other kids who had the same feelings of grief and loss.

Most of the children attending the art therapy group did not create drawings directly depicting their experience with death. They more often used color and symbols to express their feelings. At the beginning of art therapy children often used dark colors to draw monsters and other frightening images. Some scribbled in anger on their drawings.

Marc and Lara had always had access to art materials from the time they were little, drawing, painting and sculpting with plasticine almost daily. Art therapy was a natural extension of their usual self-expression. Although some bereaved children pour out their grief in their scribbled drawings, Marc's had remained placid but drabber scenes of his house, his apple tree, his swing set, and himself. Once, about six months after Don died, Lara had scribbled circles spread unevenly over a large piece of paper and instructed me to label her circles. The ones in close proximity were labeled, "Mommy," "Marc," and "Lara."

"Now write *Daddy* down in that corner"—she pointed to the circle farthest away from the cluster of three—"in case we still love him." Lara had clearly shown me her conception of death as separation.

During Lara's second year of preschool, her class was asked to draw pictures of their families. Until that assignment Lara had not used crayon and paper again to illustrate her loss. She'd just progressed from scribbling to drawing and had never attempted a realistic picture of her family before. Lara excitedly showed me her portrait the moment she stepped out of the classroom door. Her teacher smiled and remarked, "Lara handled it very well. She told me that she drew her father lying down because he was sleeping."

I wasn't sure I agreed with Lara's teacher. I didn't want Lara to connect death with sleeping, but I needn't have worried. As soon as we'd gotten home Lara had been more forthright with me. "I drew Daddy lying down sleeping because he's dead," she volunteered. I'd recognized that her still developing concept of death hadn't given her a clear picture of what Don should have looked like dead, so sleeping had been as close as she could come and still satisfy her class assignment.

Occasionally, however, a child will produce a graphic drawing of his or her loss, and Lara did just that a few weeks after starting art therapy. In her picture, she, Marc, and I were all dressed primarily in black with black tears running down our cheeks. We were a little apart from Daddy, who stood next to a sink that was outlined in black and scribbled on in brown. Daddy was dressed in black and red, the latter a color that often expresses crisis, anger, and a loss of nurturing. A red line of blood ran down Don's face. Lara entitled it, "When Daddy Died."

Eventually my children's drawings in art therapy included more bright colors and fewer browns and blacks. When the whole group was asked to draw a picture of their perfect world, Marc drew himself riding a unicorn across a brilliant rainbow, a symbol of healing.

Once a month the families of children in art therapy had an opportunity to work together during parent-child art night. One recent widow summed up the benefits very simply after she and her nine-year-old son created a serene rendition of their favorite picnic place by the lake. "We haven't had this much fun in months!"

Although process over product was emphasized in art therapy, the children's pride in their work helped nourish their self-esteem, which can be bruised by the death of a loved one. For that reason, and to reach out to the community, an art show of the children's work was displayed in a local museum.

Eventually the children in art therapy combined the arts to produce "The Circle: A Play for Children about the Circle of Life and Death," written by Dan Gray. The drama included music and dance movement that had grown out of two other specialized therapists' work with the children during regular sessions.

An innovation in the field of treatment for bereaved children, our local art therapy program inspired interest throughout the country. As yet, though, relatively few similar programs have been established elsewhere, and most surviving parents will not easily find one in their area. That doesn't mean that parents, teachers, and other adults can't use art to help a bereaved child work through the mourning process. Anyone can provide crayons and paper to children and encourage them to draw. One of the counselors who worked with the art therapy program proposed a few simple suggestions to follow when using art as a therapeutic technique.

Never interpret a child's picture for him or her; instead, use it as a cue for open-ended comments and questions such as "Tell me about your sun" or "How do you feel about your sun?"

To bridge a child's expression of feelings on paper and his or her direct expression of these feelings, ask the child, "Will you show me your sad (or angry, or embarrassed) look so I can recognize it in your picture?" Then encourage the child to make these facial expressions and join in. (This method can also be used when talking to the child.)

Just the process of doing artwork is healing because of the child's pride in creation. Praise and accept anything the child produces.

If a child is reluctant to draw, ask him or her to choose a color and scribble. Then ask the child to let the first color choose another color and make an image out of the scribble.

If a child has been encouraged to write a journal, suggest illustrating the journal as another form of self-expression.

Any form of art is a language through which children and adults can communicate their love and understanding of one another, both necessary for enabling us to support the bereaved in their journey through grief.

And so the fabric of our new life was gradually woven—the children integrated into a new school, nurtured by our church and the art therapy group, and embraced by nearby grandparents and families with other bereaved children. I had a similar network of support, a new social life, and an outreach that gave me back more than I gave to it. Although the going since Don died wasn't easy, I was relieved and also proud that the anxiety he felt near the end of his life about what would become of his wife and children proved to be unfounded. Marc and Lara turned out to be normal children—perhaps, like their father, even a touch more caring than many.

On Mother's Day at our church the children pass out flowers to their mothers and grandmothers. On the Mother's Day during our first year in Michigan Marc presented his flower to my mother and to me, but I noticed he had one more flower in his hand. I was about to chastise him for taking too many when he told me he'd gotten it for Abe to give to his mother, "because he couldn't come up and get one himself." A little boy in Marc's Sunday school class, Abe was confined to a stroller, unable to move by himself.

That same month was my great-aunt's birthday. My parents were preparing a dinner to take to her because she was too ill to come to their house as planned. I asked each of the children to draw her a birthday picture, explaining that she didn't get out much because she was old. Marc asked his grandmother, "Does she get many visitors?"

"Not many," she answered.

"Can I go to cheer her up?" he asked. And he went.

Lara has also shown the empathy of a wounded healer in outreach. When I chaperoned one of her class field trips, I was surprised to see her paired with a large, aggressive classmate whom she usually avoided. When I asked her how she ended up being the little girl's partner, she answered, "Nobody else would go with her, Mom."

Although we are a normal family, we still discuss death more than the average family would, both among ourselves and with others. When other people find out that we have suffered a loss, they often open up and talk to us. I have lectured to many groups and taught many workshops for people who need and want to know more about what it is like when a family member dies, especially for the children of the family. I have been amazed at the unfailing comfort that people give when they hear about our loss. And I have been comforted by those, even the little ones, who comfort my children.

One day Marc and his chums were playing a video game. "I got this cartridge last Christmas," Marc informed them. "It's mine."

Lara had been watching and piped up, "You used to play them with Daddy."

After a long moment of silence, Ben said, "I know how you feel, Marc, not having your dad around." Ben's father travels a lot for business.

Another friend agreed. "My dad's never around," he said.

"Is he dead?" Marc asked.

"No," the little boy answered.

"Well, my dad's really never around," Marc said, a little angered.

"But he used to be."

"Yep!" Marc said with pride. "He used to be."

The children were indeed lucky to have had Don as their father, even if the time they had with him was short. His death was an end and a beginning, not only for him, but also for us. As Don's love and support nourished us three during his lifetime, that same love, made eternal, nurtures us after his death. Marc, Lara, and I are bonded more closely together by the shared pain of his loss and by our survival and subsequent growth. I feel a confident inner strength now, something previously untested. Marc and Lara have an empathy born of the sorrow they passed through to settle into renewed happiness. Our lives go on and indeed flourish. Because Don is and always will be a very deep part of us, we can be content to live without his physical presence, even as we miss him. We have mourned together, and we will live and love together.

And we will remember his love. "Is Daddy's spirit still with us, wherever we go?" Lara asked not so very long ago.

"Yes," I answered, "but you know, you can't see it or touch it."

"I know," she said softly. "It's sort of like fresh air."

$\mathcal{A}$FTERWORD

On September 5, 1987, I married Dan Gray. Together we are blending Marc and Lara and his children, Shan, Maya, and Chay Gray, into one family.

RECOMMENDED RESOURCES

These books are some of the classics of children's books on death either because they are respected for their treatment of the subject or because the authors are widely read children's book authors. This list is by no means complete and comprehensive.

The ages given for these books are only approximate. The wonderful thing about picture books is that they appeal to all ages. Preschool children will enjoy having most of these books read to them, and they will learn from each book what they are capable of understanding. I have read *Everett Anderson's Goodbye* to high school students and watched the tears well up in their eyes. Some of these books, like *The Fall of Freddie the Leaf,* are allegories that have meaning for all.

Parents, teachers and other adults who want more information on bibliotherapy and books on death, especially for children over eight years old or for adult helpers, should consult Joanne E. Bernstein's, *Books to Help Children Cope with Separation and Loss.*

Bernstein, Joanne E., and Gullo, Stephen V. *When People Die*. New York: Dutton, 1977. The honest explanation of what happens to people when they die, both physically and spiritually, and the emotional reactions of mourning appeal to children's curiosity about death. Ages 5 and up.

Brown, Margaret Wise. *The Dead Bird*. Reading, Mass.: Addison-Wesley, 1958. After examining a dead bird for the physical symptoms of death, a group of children share a funeral for the bird, mourn and honor the creature with flowers and, eventually, forget. Ages 2–8.

Buscaglia, Leo. *The Fall of Freddie the Leaf.* Thorofare, New Jersey: Charles B. Slack, 1982. The beauty of the natural cycle of life is experienced and understood through the "eyes" of a living leaf. All ages.

Carrick, Carol. *The Accident.* New York: Clarion, 1976. A boy experiences grief's anger and sorrow when his dog is killed in a truck accident. Ages 5–8.

Clifton, Lucille. *Everett Anderson's Goodbye.* New York: Holt, Rinehart and Winston, 1983. This beautiful book illustrating the stages of grief a young boy passes through after the death of his father is the only book, to my knowledge, on the topic of parental death for very young children. Ages 3 and up.

Grollman, Earl A. *Talking About Death; A Dialogue between Parent and Child.* Boston: Beacon Press, 1976. Conversations between a parent and child about death and grief after a child's grandfather dies are followed by an explanation for parents. Ages 6–12.

Hammond, Janice M. *When My Mommy Died* and *When My Daddy Died.* Ann Arbor, Michigan: Cranbrook Publishing, 1980 and 1981. The range of feelings and fears of a grieving child are presented rather basically. These can be used as coloring books, with pages at the end for children to draw on. Ages 5–10.

Harris, Audrey. *Why Did He Die?* Minneapolis: Lerner, 1965. The rhythm of this poem about a child's friend whose grandfather dies emphasizes death as part of the cycle of nature. Ages 4–8.

Keats, Ezra Jack. *Maggie and the Pirate.* New York: Four Winds Press, 1979. Maggie's kidnapped pet cricket, killed in a fight for possession, is buried with sad songs and the chirping of other crickets. Ages 3–8.

Miles, Miska. *Annie and the Old One.* Boston: Little, Brown, 1971. A young Native American girl comes to accept the death of her grandmother with the natural philosophy of her cultural tradition. Ages 6–10.

Stein, Sara Bonnett. *About Dying: An Open Family Book for Parents and Children Together.* New York: Walker, 1974. Each picture has one text for children and one for their parents in this comprehensive, professionally prepared book. Ages 4 and up.

Viorst, Judith. *The Tenth Good Thing About Barney.* New York: Atheneum, 1971. A child eulogizes his pet at a funeral with ten good points, the last being that in death his cat will nourish life. Ages 5–9.

Zoltow, Charlotte. *My Grandson Lew.* New York: Harper and Row, 1974. A mother and her son share fond memories of his grandfather when she finally realizes that the mystified child needed to be told that the old man died. Ages 3 and up.

Although the following two books were too advanced for my children, they helped me understand my children's grief and anticipate their feelings as they grew older. They are suitable for children in late elementary grades through high school.

Krementz, Jill. *How It Feels When a Parent Dies.* New York: Knopf, 1981. Eighteen children between the ages of seven and sixteen poignantly relate their personal experiences with parental death and mourning.
LeShan, Eda. *Learning to Say Good-by: When a Parent Dies.* New York: Macmillan, 1976. A renowned psychologist reassures bereaved children and adolescents that the emotions they are feeling are perfectly normal manifestations of mourning.

The following are resources for adults, particularly professionals. Consult the bibliography for other books cited in the text.

Raymer, Mary, and McIntyre, Barbara. *The Art of Grief.* Grand Traverse Area Hospice, 1105 Sixth Street, Traverse City, MI 49684, 1986. (A videotape of *The Circle: A Play for Children about the Circle of Life and Death* by Dan Gray is also available from the above address.)
Rudolph, Marguerita. *Should the Children Know?, Encounters with Death in the Lives of Children.* New York: Schocken Books, 1978. This book shares the experience of a teacher helping her class and their parents accept the death of a classmate.
THEOS, a network of support for widowed men and women and their families, 1301 Clark Building, 717 Liberty Avenue, Pittsburgh, PA 15222.

BIBLIOGRAPHY

Bernstein, Joanne E. *Books to Help Children Cope with Separation and Loss*. New York: R. R. Bowker Co., 1983.

Bowlby, John. *Attachment and Loss, Volumes I–III*. New York: Basic Books, 1969, 1973, 1980.

Caine, Lynn. *Widow*. New York: William Morrow & Co., Inc., 1974.

Furman, Erna. *A Child's Parent Dies*. New Haven, Conn.: Yale University Press, 1967.

Grollman, Earl A. *Talking About Death: A Dialogue Between Parent and Child*. Boston: Beacon Press, 1967.

Jewett, Claudia L. *Helping Children Cope with Separation and Loss*. Harvard, Mass.: Harvard Common Press, 1982.

Klopfenstein, Janette. *Tell Me about Death, Mommy*. Scottdale, Pa.: Herald Press, 1977.

Kübler-Ross, Elisabeth. *On Death and Dying*. New York: Macmillan, 1969.

Nouwen, Henri J. M. *The Wounded Healer*. Garden City, N.Y.: Image Books, 1972.

Piaget, Jean. *The Language and Thought of the Child*. New York: Meridan Books, 1955.

Wolfenstein, Martha, and Kliman, Gilbert, eds. *Children and the Death of a President*. Garden City, N.Y.: Doubleday, 1965.